LIVING TRANSLATION
THEIR STORIES

LIVING TRANSLATION
THEIR STORIES

DR. BRUCE A. SMITH

XULON PRESS

Xulon Press
2301 Lucien Way #415
Maitland, FL 32751
407.339.4217
www.xulonpress.com

Unless otherwise indicated, Scripture quotations are taken from the Holy Bible, New International Version, © 1973, 1978, 1984, 2011 by The International Bible Society. Used by permission of Zondervan Bible Publishers.

Printed in the United States of America.

ISBN-13: 9781545612309

TABLE OF CONTENTS

INTRODUCTION

During the past two years, I have often reflected on the account in John 9 of Jesus's miraculous healing of the man born blind. This may seem an odd devotional, but I have spent much of my life praying for a miracle—and God has answered. In fact, He is still answering miraculously. I am a witness to it. But, like the neighbors who witnessed the blind man's healing, I find myself unprepared for God's answer and uncertain how to describe the miracle.

Perhaps this is because miracles, by definition, are rare. They are extraordinary. They are unbelievable. They defy rational explanation. Claiming to have witnessed a miracle is to invite disbelief and derision, even from those who also believe in and pray for miracles. Our practical theology of miracles has become "that which does not occur."

But God's ways are not our ways. We see blindness as a limitation. Jesus described the man's blindness as an opportunity to display the work of God in his life. In a very unexpected and simple way, Jesus did the impossible. He gave the blind man sight.

The reaction of the man's neighbors and family are like my own—denial, confusion, speculation, investigation, and distraction. Yet the blind man sees.

I have been praying that God would move His Church worldwide to become active stewards of His Word in every language. I'm not at all sure how I imagined God might do this. I suppose deep down I didn't believe He would do it. It would require a miracle.

The global Church is so diverse, facing so many challenges, and divided along countless cultural fault lines. Regard for Scripture is waning in the West, while Scripture in European languages continues to rule much of the rest of the world. The Reformation, with its accompanying translation of the Bible from Latin into local languages, impacted Europe five centuries ago. But for more than six thousand languages worldwide the Reformation is someone else's history. Their Bible is in someone else's language.

During the past ninety years, Bible translation ministries have made significant progress. Before 1900 the full Bible had been translated into fewer than twenty languages. At the time of this writing, the complete Bible has been translated into more than 630 languages. Much of this progress is due to the sacrificial life's work of cross-cultural missionaries moving from "the West to the rest" during the mid-twentieth century. This model is sometimes described as "one translator, one language, one lifetime." The opening of the twenty-first century has seen these pioneering translators retiring in record numbers.

Fortunately, the result of twentieth-century missions has been the spread of Christianity globally. First, second, and third generation Christians are leading churches and mission organizations throughout the South and East, continuing the work of their spiritual predecessors. Their proximity to Bibleless peoples, and their multi-lingual experience, has enabled them to accelerate and extend Bible translation far beyond its former reach. Bible translations are currently in progress in more than 2,700 languages worldwide.

But more than half of the world's languages are still without a single verse of Scripture. It would take a miracle, or perhaps many miracles, to translate the Bible into all of these languages in our lifetime.

These miracles are happening today in hundreds of languages worldwide. These are just a few of their stories.

DEDICATION

This book is dedicated to hundreds of millions of people who are still waiting for God's Word in their heart language, and to everyone who is working to get His Word to them.

ACKNOWLEDGEMENTS

This book is an attempt to give voice to hundreds of language groups, and millions of people, whose voices are too seldom heard. In order to faithfully capture their words I spent a lot of time listening, asking questions, and soliciting their editorial input. My sincere desire is to faithfully communicate their stories in a way that respects their history and journey as stewards of God's Word in their nations and languages. Some of these stories are connected explicitly to individuals involved. This was only done with their permission. I am acutely aware of the risks that speaking up creates for them, and I do not want to add to their difficulties. They are already facing more challenges than they should in this work. In cases where attributing stories to individuals would put them at undue risk, I have used pseudonyms or left out their names. Thanks to each of these partners for translating their faith and regard for God's Word into action every day.

The rapidly expanding number of Wycliffe Associates staff and volunteers serving on MAST teams means that most of them remain anonymous. I did not want to fill these pages with lists of names of people that the reader will likely never meet. At the same time, I tried to include personal stories of some of those involved in order to add depth to the accounts. In every chapter, nation, and event described there are many more people who contributed to the success and progress of Bible translation. Their crowns will be laid at Jesus's feet. For now, I can only express my deepest respect and appreciation for their partnership in advancing Bible translation. They have impacted millions of people as ambassadors for Christ.

At the outset of this writing project, I knew that I was considering a task too large for me to accomplish in a timely fashion without significant help. The amount of research required was daunting. Since coming to Wycliffe Associates in 2000, our daughters have been intimately involved in the ministry as volunteers, donors, and prayer partners. Someday they will write their own stories of life and ministry. Our oldest daughter, Abby, assisted with this book. She personally interviewed many of the MAST team members. On the day of her first interview, she felt Satan's opposition personally as she was struck with an atypical migraine. At first we thought she was having a stroke, but by God's grace He kept her from greater harm and enabled her to continue working on this book. Abby also provided unflinching editorial feedback to sharpen my writing. She's a skilled writer and editor, she knows international ministry from her own life experiences, and she obviously knows me well. It has been a profound blessing for me to collaborate with Abby in writing this book.

Two others deserve my appreciation for their editorial feedback. Because Dan Kramer lived most of these stories personally, his investment in accurately telling these stories was essential. He provided feedback to every chapter while in the midst of leading our MAST team creating new stories every day worldwide. Someday he will write his story as well. Another member of our MAST team, Tabitha Price, also contributed tremendously valuable editorial feedback. Having grown up on the mission field, and around Bible translation her entire life, Tabitha brought helpful perspective to communicate clearly and effectively in these stories.

Thanks to Cindy Gray for, again, lending her creative talents to create a book cover that complements the contents.

Despite the best efforts of all of these people, errors may have inadvertently found their way into my writing. For that, I accept sole responsibility and apologize in advance.

ENDORSEMENTS

"*Great and successful work demands the greatest collaboration. With sincerity and distinctiveness, Bruce sheds light on a new model of Bible translation (MAST) with its heart set on engaging local churches practically in the translation work in order to finish the task of Bible translation in the world. The book includes interesting stories of the individual work on practical translation engagement in different localities across the globe. These are live testimonies that call for attention to engage the masses, speed the work of translation, and maintain its quality to the highest standards. MAST is a must if we consider Bible translation as a mission to reach the lost and to nurture believers. I hope this book would inspire many people to join the Bible translation movement, and speed God's Word to the nations.*"

– Woyita W. Olla, Ph.D.
Chairman of Wycliffe Ethiopia Board
Deputy General Secretary of the
Ethiopian Kale Heywet Church

"*Wycliffe Philippines had been asking the question in light of the advancement of human capacity, knowledge, and technology: is there no better way other than ten, twenty or thirty years to translate God's Word in all the known and unknown languages of the nations? The answer came through MAST, and we took this by the horn—believing and understanding the philosophical and methodological underpinnings of this new approach to Bible translation. More than that, I see*"

MAST at the core of the Great Commission of our Lord Jesus. By empowering and equipping the nations to take ownership in translating God's Word in their heart language, we are contributing to making disciples of all nations. A new dawn in missions has come, the nations are taking God's Word to the nations; this is Great Commission Bible Translation. I am convinced that we have an unprecedented opportunity in our lifetime to see the Bible translated into all the languages of the world, thereby hastening the coming of the End so that the Gospel of the Kingdom will be preached in all the world as a witness to the nations. Maranatha!"

– Rev. Romerlito C. Macalinao, Ed.D.
Executive Director/CEO of Wycliffe Philippines

"Living Translation' takes you on an exciting journey revealing how God is using ordinary people and communities around the world to translate the Bible for their own people for the very first time. This eloquent, simple, and yet poignant account of the revolution taking place in the world of Bible translation will challenge and inspire you. A real treasure of a book."

– Efi Tembon
General Director of the Cameroon Association
for Bible Translation and Literacy (CABTAL)

Chapter One

HIGH MOUNTAINS

I f the Bible included photos, we might find a picture of
the Ng people to illustrate the definition of the least of
these. They live in the remote mountains of South Asia.
Official research indicates there are just a few thousand Ng
speakers, and they are dying out. Apparently, the Ng didn't

get that memo. They report 30,000 speakers and growing. Ng has not been a written language, only spoken until a secular organization recently began developing an alphabet. They live simply as they have for generations. They cause no one trouble and are ignored as a result. The Ng are traditionally Animists, but some have become Christians through the witness of pastors in the area. There are just four Christian churches among their villages. Scripture is often read from a Bible in the majority language that was translated more than one hundred years ago.

The Ng were on no one's priority list for Bible translation.

But in a nearby language group, a local man translated the New Testament into his language. They had fewer Christians than the Ng, but they had Scripture in their own language. Ng believers heard of other nearby languages where Bible translation was also in progress. This stirred a vision and hope to have God's Word in Ng. They prayed for God to show them the way.

A Winding Path

Dan Kramer was teaching English as a Second Language (ESL) during the day at a middle school and in the evenings at Wayne State University in suburban Detroit. The community served by the middle school included thirty-eight languages. Over time the local population was increasingly comprised of refugees from war-torn countries. It was challenging and rewarding work.

For their tenth anniversary Dan and his wife, Holly, decided to vacation in Orlando, Florida. After enjoying a few days at the local attractions they checked out of their hotel but had most of the day to fill before their return flight departed. As Christians they were aware of, and curious about, missions. So, when they saw an advertisement for tours of the Jesus Film offices and Bible Translation Discovery Center they thought this would be a good way to spend their last hours in Orlando. The timing didn't work for the Jesus Film tour, so Dan and Holly showed up at the Bible Translation Discovery Center with little idea what to expect.

As they toured, they learned about the challenges and opportunities of Bible translation. One section highlighted language learning and linguistics, which immediately resonated with Dan because of his teaching background. In a moment, what had been detached entertainment turned into a personal reflection on why God was showing him this new perspective. Before he left Dan filled out a contact card requesting more information, sensing that God was calling him—but to what, he was unsure.

After returning to Detroit, Dan and Holly returned to their routines and caring for their growing family. The momentary tug on Dan's heart faded in his memory until the phone rang one day. A recruiter from Wycliffe Associates was calling. Dan's first response was to cut the salesman off. But the recruiter simply said, "Don't worry, we only want you to join us when God wants you to. I'm just getting information and asking if you would like information from us by email." "Sure, no problem," Dan answered, reminding himself—*my computer's 'delete' button works just fine.*

Almost four years later Dan was in his classroom when he received an email from Wycliffe Associates describing a volunteer opportunity in the High Mountains that caught his attention. Instead of deleting the email, Dan responded and signed up for the trip, not even sure what he would be doing.

Dan was part of a team that provided a Vacation Bible School program for missionary kids while their parents attended annual Bible translation planning meetings. He roomed with a missionary from India and learned about the urgent needs for Bible translation there. The needs gripped his heart, but he was unsure how to add more commitments to his already full life. So, Dan began bargaining with God about the implications for his family. The next morning the team leader asked Dan whether he would be interested in starting a program teaching English to international partners in Bible translation. Dan was shocked but secretly hopeful that maybe God wasn't calling him to move to India.

During the next year, Dan considered the possibility of seasonal involvement teaching English Language Learning (ELL) for Bible translators but soon realized that this was a half-hearted response. He and Holly talked about moving their family to Florida to join Wycliffe Associates full-time. They made the decision, sold their home in the midst of a national economic crisis, and moved to Orlando in July of 2010.

Five years after Dan filled out the information card, he was flying to South Korea to launch the ELL program for their Bible translators. During the next three years this program grew to a staff of thirty, and more than two hundred volunteers, serving Bible translation partners in thirty countries. Most training and reference resources for Bible translation have historically been in English, so improving English language competency increases translators' access to valuable tools. Clearly, the English Language Learning program was meeting an urgent need in Bible translation worldwide.

No one had any idea what God had in mind for the future.

Providential Meetings

One of the English Language Learning team members was a young American girl named Kaitlin. As she became involved teaching ELL in the High Mountains she worked closely with the national staff and learned about the unique challenges and opportunities for Bible translation in the region. One of the young men she met, Jeewan, was the son of the Bible translator in the language near the Ng people. Over time their mutual admiration turned to love and commitment and they were married.

During this time Jeewan had been an ELL student, experiencing the unique impact of the teaching method Dan used. It made sense to him. It matched his way of thinking and learning. It also began stirring a question deep in Jeewan's heart and mind. For his entire life, he had seen the impact of the "one translator, one language, one lifetime" model in his country. His heart was broken for those still without Scripture after so many years.

In late 2013 Dan led an ELL training workshop in Orlando that Jeewan attended. Jeewan asked Dan a question that had been weighing on him. "Could you use this ELL training method to help us improve Bible translation?"

The question caught Dan by surprise. His first thought was that Jeewan knew much more about Bible translation than he did. So, he asked Jeewan to teach him their current model for Bible translation. Dan took copious notes from their conversations and studied them intently in the weeks that followed.

As Dan reviewed his notes one particular statement caught his attention. "Church checking six months later." It was Jeewan's description of getting church input on the translation drafts. Dan was thinking like a teacher, wondering how students would feel if their work wasn't graded for six months. Would they even remember why they answered a certain way? What Dan didn't understand was that checking in six months was extraordinarily fast in the High Mountains. To him, the delay contradicted what he knew about language learning theory and practice.

Late one night Dan rolled out a length of butcher paper and drew a new translation workflow that included all of the essential translation elements that Jeewan had described, but with quality checking integrated throughout the process. He estimated how many verses a translator could draft <u>and</u> check in a day, and calculated how long it would take to complete a New Testament in this model. Based on his assumptions it should take just forty months! This was about three times faster than the typical pace of translation in the High Mountains. Dan was shocked.

The next morning Dan briefly reviewed his midnight scribblings with Jeewan. Jeewan responded enthusiastically, "That's what we want!" The timing was providential, as Dan had a meeting with me later that day to discuss the future direction of the English Language Learning program.

During our meeting, Dan provided an in-depth review of the scope, depth, and impact of the ELL program. Among the many PowerPoint slides was a single slide describing the question Jeewan had asked. At first, Dan thought it had escaped my attention. It had not. I had no idea of the implications, but because it had been raised by one of our international partners I encouraged Dan to do research and a field test. In Dan's version of this conversation he quotes me saying, "Money is no object." I have no memory of that statement, and deny ever saying it. Nonetheless, Dan moved forward in faith.

He explained his ideas to a few others in Wycliffe Associates and asked for their input. In early 2014 he formed a team of translation consultants, university educators, and a Biblical language expert, to convert his butcher paper and notes into a workshop curriculum that could be implemented and evaluated. Plans, and prayer, aimed toward a test in the High Mountains in June 2014. The workshop was named Mobilized Assistance Supporting Translation—MAST for short.

The workshop design called for two weeks of training followed by two weeks of translation and community checking. Progress estimates were recalculated based on the input from the broader team, and Dan was speechless. What had recently appeared to require forty months to translate a full New Testament could potentially be done by a larger translation team in just forty weeks! He wisely kept this quiet, knowing others would think he had lost his mind.

The First Test of MAST

In the High Mountains, Jeewan invited four experienced Bible translation teams, with two translators on each team, to participate in the June 2014 MAST workshop. These teams had attended previous translation training workshops and were all making slow and steady progress on translating the New Testament into their heart languages. One team had already drafted their entire New Testament except for 1 and 2 Thessalonians. These were the books chosen for the first MAST test.

The first two weeks of training included daily teaching and discussion on subjects including translation principles, Biblical Greek, drafting and writing, critical thinking skills, and back-translating. The content was challenging, but appreciated by every team. At the end of two weeks, the teams took a weekend break in the mountains to clear their heads and rest up for the week of translation ahead.

That weekend Dan gathered his facilitation team together for a meal and handed out a one and a half page summary of the MAST translation process they would put to the test on Monday morning. Dan was suddenly self-conscious about the simplicity of what he was proposing. The team glanced briefly at the pages, then moved quickly on to ice cream.

On Monday morning the translation teams met together for worship and prayer. Soon they were ready to dive into translating. Dan described the eight steps of MAST to the entire group:

1. Read the chapter in a related language.
2. Discuss the chapter in your own language.
3. Chunk = divide the chapter into small portions of a few related verses.
4. Blind draft = close your Bible and translate each chunk from short-term memory.
5. Self-check = check your translation against the source and edit for accuracy.
6. Peer check = check your teammate's translation against the source and agree upon edits.
7. Keyword check = check key theological terms to assure accuracy and consistency.
8. Verse by verse check = review of every verse in context.

The four translation teams moved into separate rooms to begin working. Dan moved from room to room to observe how they accomplished each of the eight steps. Each team had their own style of working, but they were all following the steps. As Dan observed he received feedback as each team worked. One group soon became very frustrated. Another group was struggling, clearly hesitant to follow a translation method that was different from what they had previously learned and used. The other two groups complied with the MAST steps but increasingly questioned it in comparison to their previous translation methods.

Blind drafting was uncomfortable for all of them. They were used to translating with continuous reference to the source texts and were tangibly afraid that they would make mistakes if they didn't consult the reference while writing. Fears turned to whispers, and whispers to murmurs by mid-afternoon Monday. Dan encouraged them to follow the MAST steps.

After the day's work, Dan told the teams a story about John Dewey, an American educational innovator. Dewey had created something called a Laboratory School. The idea was to continuously experiment and test new ways of teaching and learning while students were educated in their normal subjects. Initially, his idea met criticism, but over time it proved that both teaching and learning could improve significantly over the common methods. Experimenting with different teaching models led to improved learning. Dan related this model to the first day of their experience with MAST. He thanked them for trying and assured them that things would improve the next day.

As the facilitation team met after dinner, Dan said, "Stay the course." His sense was that they needed to improve their communication with the translation teams, not change the MAST method.

On Tuesday morning the improvement was immediately apparent. Shortly after getting to work one of the translation teams burst into laughter that everyone in the building could hear. Dan went to investigate. They were well into chapter two and reviewing it together. Laughter had replaced the stress of the previous day. One said, "I don't know how everyone doesn't see that this method is better!" As Dan moved to the second group he could tell they were more optimistic, even though less expressive. They could see the improvement in drafting but had not begun quality checking yet. The third team said, "All our concerns have been answered." With increasing confidence, Dan moved on to the fourth team. They were still frustrated, and Dan's presence only increased their stress. This pattern continued for the rest of Tuesday.

On Wednesday a nasty germ got the best of Dan and put him flat on his back. The facilitation team continued encouraging the translation teams, but as three teams gained momentum, the fourth remained mired in frustration. At the end of the day, Dan asked the facilitators to switch translation teams hoping that a change in communication and facilitation might help the fourth team break through as the others had.

Thursday started promisingly, both for the translation teams and for Dan.

The Ng Arrive

Around morning tea break two new men arrived at the workshop. They were Ng. They had walked for two days and had nothing but the clothes on their backs. They wanted a Bible translation. They were not translators, and had missed all of the training as well as the first three days of using MAST methodology. The only reasonable response would be to send them away. Instead, Dan took another step of faith and said, "Let's get started."

Immediately Dan realized he had another complication—all of his facilitators were already working with the other teams. That left him to work with the Ng. Now the person who had pushed everyone else out of their comfort zones was as nervous as they were!

Dan began coaching the Ng team after lunch. They divided 1 Thessalonians chapter 1 into chunks and followed his instructions perfectly. Each man made blind drafts, then self-checked and edited to assure that everything in the source was in the translation. Then they traded papers and checked each other's work. At this point, Dan suggested that they read their translation out loud.

The elder read aloud while the younger listened. Naturally, Dan couldn't understand a word. But as the younger man listened tears welled up in his eyes. Dan froze in place and whispered a prayer. He called one of the experienced translation consultants over to check the quality of their work. They spent the next four hours talking about the chapter. At the end of the discussion, the consultant's evaluation shocked everyone. "Their translation is as good as the other teams'."

What? They missed the training. They have no translation experience.

What does this mean?

What just happened?

More Important Questions

Based on the results of their initial translation, Dan encouraged the Ng team to continue. In the days that followed, the Ng team completed drafting and checking 1 Thessalonians while the other teams completed both 1 and 2 Thessalonians. The work of all the teams was quality checked by two experienced Bible translation consultants. All of the teams and translators agreed that MAST produced an accurate and more natural sounding translation than their previous methods.

The translation quality and pace confirmed the validity of the MAST method. The experienced translation teams made plans to integrate MAST into their ongoing translation work. But the Ng wanted more. They wanted the entire New Testament as soon as possible.

"How many people should we bring to translate the whole New Testament?" The Ng men didn't know how outrageous their question was. They only knew how desperately they wanted God's Word for their families and neighbors.

After some calculations Dan responded, "How about twenty-six translators for two weeks?" Based on the pace of translation at this first workshop, the average translator was drafting <u>and</u> checking thirty-one verses per day. Twenty-six people, each working at this pace for ten days, would complete the New Testament and allow for a slight margin for distractions. Plus, the Ng had already completed 1 Thessalonians!

The Ng translators agreed, then turned to start the long walk home. Their plan was to recruit enough translators to complete their New Testament by the end of the year.

The Shock

I was traveling to visit Wycliffe Associates ministry partners around the U.S. when that first MAST workshop was underway. I remember receiving the email report of the workshop results from Dan. It was unbelievable. My first thought was that Dan was exaggerating. I didn't know what to make of his report. Then I received a second report from another member of the facilitation team, Wycliffe Associates'

Vice-President of Recruiting. Deborah confirmed the unbelievable news.

After a few email exchanges, I was still in shock. The next time Facebook asked me to post what I was thinking I posed this question, "How many translators would it take to translate the entire New Testament in two weeks?" Naturally, in my circle of friends, this generated a fair amount of comments and conversation. I had no idea how shocking that question would be to people working in the "one translator, one language, one lifetime" model.

Fall Ng MAST

As the Ng Christians arrived in November for the second workshop, Dan quickly realized they did not have twenty-six translators. They had come with thirteen. One of the foundational principles of MAST is to trust God's preparation and provision through the local church. When our expectations aren't met, or our plans don't work out, we choose to trust God's plan. The Ng team included elders and youth, pastors and farmers, men and women, mature Christians and new Christians. One man had been possessed by demons for most of his lifetime. One of the young women was the only Christian in her village. Her mother had disappeared in the mountains years before, so she was raising her younger brother and sister. Her nearest Christian neighbor was a two-hour walk from her village. Each of them was chosen to participate by their church leaders.

As the workshop opened Dan gave an overview of the process. The Ng team listened quietly and respectfully. Only one man was willing to voice his uncertainty. "Who are we to translate God's Word?" As Dan paused to formulate a reassurance one of the High Mountain facilitators asked to respond. He had been among the most skeptical at the beginning of the June MAST workshop but had become a passionate advocate for MAST by the end of that workshop. His testimony reassured the Ng team members in a way that Dan could not.

After the orientation, Dan and the facilitation team assessed the Ng team members' multilingual language abilities, Biblical knowledge, critical thinking, and computer skills. Based on this information the Ng were divided into four teams matched with the translation difficulty of Matthew, Mark, Luke, and John. With no preconceived ideas or other models of translation to follow they enthusiastically launched into the eight-step MAST process to translate the gospels.

While Dan and his team began the second MAST workshop I stayed in the U.S. until Thanksgiving was over, then flew to join them. I needed to see MAST firsthand in order to get over my own skepticism. When I arrived at the workshop at the beginning of the second week all of the Westerners were standing out on the driveway with their arms folded. At first I didn't know what to make of it, but when I got out of the car I realized they were just trying to keep warm in the sun. At that time of year it is very cold in the mountains. The workshop location had no central heating system, so everyone soaked up every ray of sunshine and drank as much tea, coffee, and hot chocolate as they could hold.

"You missed it," Dan said as I walked up. "Missed what?" I responded. By the third day of the workshop the local people were managing every detail themselves. The Westerners had already worked themselves out of a job. I have to say that after hearing this vision described in mission circles for thirty years it was exciting to see it happening!

Progress was steadily being made. Each translator spent the first couple of hours each day drafting the day's assignment. By the time morning tea was ready, checking was already in full swing. Every member of the Ng team was working energetically, engaging in discussion with their teammates on translation challenges, and prayerfully checking one another's work.

Even though the Ng language had been unwritten until just recently, the Ng translators adopted the newly developed alphabet despite its limited usage. However, because they had never spelled Ng words before there were vigorous debates on the proper spelling of many words. It was exciting to watch them debating spelling for the first time in their history!

After a full day of checking their gospels, the Ng gathered together after dinner for discussion of key theological terms and for the public reading of their translations. As individuals stood to read the gospels the room was silent—everyone in rapt attention. The pastors led discussions comparing differences between parables told in multiple gospels. It was the first time in their history that the entire Bible reading, study, and discussion was in their heart language.

I groped for words to describe what I was witnessing. As I wrote an email to my family later that night I found the right word, "Miraculous!"

Final Report

In these two weeks the Ng translators drafted <u>and</u> checked Matthew, Mark, Luke, John, and 1 and 2 Timothy—49 percent of the New Testament! Because their goal was to complete their New Testament, I sometimes describe this facetiously as a shocking failure—only completing <u>half</u> the New Testament in two weeks!

Because they didn't finish their New Testament at the end of 2014, the Ng regrouped in 2015 to complete their translation. They ultimately completed their New Testament within a year of beginning their translation. They submitted their translation for review by others to confirm the accuracy, sent it for typesetting and printing, and celebrated the dedication in the fall of 2016.

As the workshop ended there was tremendous celebration for what God had accomplished through His Ng church to get His Word to their people. Christians from other language groups, some with Scripture and some still without, were invited to join in this celebration. I struggled to describe the implications of what had happened there in terms of the hope and opportunity their steps of faith would give to others still without Scripture. I had no idea what God had in store for the future but I knew that what the Ng had accomplished could change the future of Bible translation worldwide. By faith, they had done something that would strengthen the faith of others and encourage them to take similar steps.

Chapter Two

MYANMAR

For most of my life Myanmar, also known as Burma, has been overlooked—not only by me but also by most of the Western world. Other nations in Southeast Asia captured the headlines during my childhood. Vietnam, Laos, and Cambodia were in the news. As the fog of the Vietnam

War dissipated, China loomed ever larger on the Asian horizon. Japan and North and South Korea faded in my vague understanding of twentieth-century history. Asia seemed very far away.

When Jan and I joined Mission Aviation Fellowship (MAF) we heard about Indonesia, but we were assigned to serve in South America. So it wasn't until I became Chief Operating Officer for MAF that I gave any serious thought to the ministry needs in Asia. Myanmar surfaced during our global ministry assessment we did in the early 1990s. I remember having brief conversations about Myanmar with our international MAF partners and learning that MAF-UK was planning to establish a base there. With other strategic priorities on the horizon, I lost sight of Myanmar for the next twenty years.

As I came to Wycliffe Associates I soon realized that Asia has more people without Scripture than any other region in the world. Within Asia, Myanmar ranked fifth in population without Scripture. It was time to pay more attention.

History

Southeast Asia is a region of tremendous cultural diversity. Myanmar is bordered by India to the west, China to the north, and Laos and Thailand to the east. Tropical coastal jungles bordered by high mountain ranges to the north slowed but didn't actually stop outside conquests. Invaders from South China, and later from Mongolia, overpowered the Burmese people at various times in their history. The local people have had to battle for freedom from foreign domination repeatedly.

In 1812 Adoniram Judson and his wife, Nancy, were sent from the fledgling United States as Christian missionaries to Burma. They spent the first three years immersed in learning the language. Nancy focused on becoming a fluent conversationalist. Adoniram studied Burmese grammar and vocabulary in preparation for translating the Bible. Above and beyond the challenges of local language and culture was the Burmese law, prescribing death to anyone changing their religion from Hinduism or Buddhism. Not surprisingly, conversions to Christianity were few. Judson first published the Gospel of Matthew in 1817. It would be two more years before one person converted to Christianity. In 1823 he completed the Burmese New Testament translation. At that point, the Burmese church numbered eighteen believers.

The next year British colonial powers began a series of wars with Burma over territory and resources. Adoniram was soon arrested by the British forces on suspicion of collaboration with the Burmese. He spent the next seventeen months imprisoned in the most brutal conditions. Britain finally overpowered the Burmese army in 1826 and released Judson from his imprisonment. Nancy died soon after, but Adoniram pressed on to evangelize the Burmese people.

A major breakthrough came among the Karen people, a minority ethnic group in eastern Burma whose religious beliefs and oral traditions had prepared them to receive the gospel. Judson's translation of the complete Bible in Burmese was published in 1835, further facilitating the spread of the gospel. By the time of his death in 1850, there were more than one hundred churches and eight thousand believers. Judson's translation remains the most popular Bible in Myanmar—180 years later.

First Steps

In 2010 Wycliffe Associates looked for ways to support Bible translation in Myanmar. We learned of a partner that was beginning translation in a very remote region of the country. The security situation there was sensitive, so our contact with the translators was only through intermediaries. We had limited information about their progress. All of this made it very difficult for us to raise funding for their support. As this discussion surfaced with our Wycliffe Associates board of directors, several board members made the decision to sponsor this Bible translation effort personally. Their steps of faith encouraged us to explore further.

The next few years were a season of significant political change in Myanmar. Hundreds of political prisoners were released and granted amnesty. Freedom of the press increased. Democratic elections in 2012 gave the National League for Democracy dozens of seats in the parliament.

The political climate in Myanmar improved dramatically, opening new opportunities for ministry partnerships with Burmese churches. Because many Burmese languages are unwritten, our next step was to build a recording studio in central Myanmar to record, reproduce, and distribute Scripture translations in audio formats.

During the fall of 2014, Wycliffe Associates' Asia team gathered in Myanmar to discuss strategies for advancing Bible translation in the region. Dan Kramer attended the meeting and described the emerging MAST strategy. Already facing many challenges in the region, the team was anxious to see whether MAST might overcome some of the difficulties.

As our Asia team began networking to identify potential locations for MAST, Myanmar was naturally part of the discussion. In neighboring India, our ELL team had connected with a young Burmese Christian, Isaac Pai, who was doing language surveys. We asked Isaac if he would be willing to assist as an interpreter for our team at a meeting to introduce MAST to Burmese church leaders. Isaac enthusiastically agreed and began networking with church leaders and his university classmates back in Myanmar to rally support for the effort.

Introducing MAST

Leaders from churches in several different languages were invited to attend the introductory MAST meeting in October 2014. Mike Hatfield, Dan's former pastor and now a partner in ELL and MAST, led the meeting. Isaac was Mike's interpreter. Prior to this meeting, MAST had only been tested in one workshop in the High Mountains in June 2014. Mike was a facilitator in that initial MAST workshop, but with very limited experience our team was climbing a steep learning curve.

Mike explained the MAST Bible translation method and described what he had seen God do through the local translators in the High Mountains. The Burmese church leaders asked a lot of questions. Then, Mike invited them to try MAST translation for themselves. As they followed the eight steps their understanding and excitement began to build. After a few days of discussion, translation experience, and prayer the Burmese church leaders agreed that MAST was the best way for them to get Scripture to their people. Planning immediately began for a two-week multi-language MAST workshop in February 2015.

Thirty-three churches, from ten different language groups, sent translators to the first Burmese MAST workshop. Pause. Breathe that in. Read it again.

Forty translators, working in ten languages, spent two weeks together. They worshiped, prayed, studied, sang, ate, laughed, lived, and worked together. They encouraged one another. They challenged one another. And during the workshop they translated the book of Mark for their own languages—for the first time in history!

The workshop concluded with a time of worship and celebration. As the translators returned to their homes and churches, their vision and plan was to complete their New Testament translations in the coming year.

Caring for Quality

Accuracy is vital in Bible translation. Everyone agrees. MAST integrates checking throughout the process, so quality is a priority from the very start of the translation. Then, as the translation is circulated within the church and community, additional feedback surfaces. Often this relates to format, spelling, or dialect differences. Sometimes it relates to misunderstandings about the meaning of a passage. Sometimes a Scripture passage is inherently difficult to understand. The good news is that all of this creates dialog and discussion within the church to assure that everyone understands the meaning—especially when it is difficult to understand.

After continuing their translations following the workshop, the Burmese church leaders asked to gather together again specifically to discuss quality assurance. Our MAST team responded by organizing a quality checking workshop for them in October of 2015. Due to visa complications, our facilitators actually made two round-trips from the U.S. to Myanmar. The first time, they were turned back at the airport. They came back to the U.S., sorted out the visa issues with the Myanmar Consulate in Washington, DC, then boarded another flight to get back to Myanmar for the workshop! Seven of the original ten language groups were able to attend. One of the language groups sent twenty-two people to participate in the workshop!

During the morning group devotion one of our MAST facilitators, Robert Harmon, felt led by the Holy Spirit to reflect on Acts 4:13. "When they saw the courage of Peter and John and realized that they were unschooled, ordinary men, they were astonished and they took note that these men had been with Jesus."

The most profound discovery for these Burmese church leaders was realizing that God had already equipped them uniquely to evaluate the quality of Bible translation in their heart languages. They are instruments in God's hands, with a lifetime of knowledge of their language and culture, and discernment from the Holy Spirit—to steward God's Word for their people. They have access to tools, research, and resources to assist them in their work. As they reviewed the work of their translation teams, they realized again that it is *God's Word*. He is sovereign over it, and He works through His people to guard and guide its translation.

MAST Momentum

Following the quality checking workshop, momentum built. Over the next six months, there was a MAST workshop in Myanmar every month. This was possible because Isaac recruited a team of Burmese facilitators to serve at these workshops.

The Daa Yindu translators attended the MAST introduction, the first MAST workshop, and the quality checking workshop. They completed translating the four gospels but were ready to move forward more rapidly. In December 2015 they brought forty-two translators to a MAST workshop— and finished the rest of their New Testament! Our MAST team brought a desktop printer to the workshop, and every translator went home with their own copy of the Daa Yindu New Testament! What a celebration!

The Taiphun people sent five people to observe the Daa Yindu translators. While they were observing, the Taiphun translated Mark and 1 & 2 Thessalonians. When they went home they invited others to join the translation team and completed the rest of their New Testament at their next MAST workshop!

One of the Burmese facilitators at the Daa Yindu workshop said, "My language, Tapong, doesn't have the Bible yet." So, he went home and recruited twenty-six translators for their own MAST workshop in February 2016. The Tapong were the first people in the world to translate, and quality check, their entire New Testament in two weeks!

Khawng Tu

Among the first groups that attended the MAST introduction, and the quality checking workshop, were translators from a very remote minority group—the Khawng Tu. Their language is not recognized by the government. It is not recognized in linguistic research. They say they have been ignored and overlooked for generations. They say, "In the world's eyes, we are no one."

Khawng Tu was an unwritten language until they began translating their New Testament in 2014. As they considered their options, they decided that the Roman alphabet matched their language better than the Burmese letters. So, they began spelling their words using the modern alphabet.

By the time they came to the quality checking workshop in the fall of 2015 they had translated portions of their New Testament—using only pen and paper. They had no access to computers in their communities. During the workshop, a discussion began about translating the Old Testament. For these believers, the New Testament was simply the starting point. They wanted the entire Bible. As they considered the challenge of the Old Testament, with almost three times the content as the New Testament, they realized they would need even more translators. Someone suggested it might require one hundred translators to translate the Old Testament. The Khawng Tu leaders spoke up, "We can do it!"

The Khawng Tu were committed to completing their New Testament before beginning their Old Testament. They made plans for their Old Testament MAST workshop to be in April 2016 and set to work to complete their New Testament before that date. When word of their plans spread, several of us at Wycliffe Associates decided we wanted to be a part of this historic effort. The Wycliffe Associates Board Chair, Kris Rinne, joined the MAST facilitation team. Jan and I were traveling in Armenia when the workshop began, but we joined the workshop for the second week. Brent Ropp, Vice-President of Operations, and Tim Neu, Vice-President of Finance, also added Myanmar to their travel schedules.

By the time we arrived the MAST workshop was a beehive of activity. The Khawng Tu had mobilized 117 translators to translate their Old Testament! This included seventeen pastors. Isaac recruited his mother and aunt to cook for everyone! The translators ate in shifts as the cooks completed each course of the meals.

In the preceding months, they had completed their New Testament translation in manuscript! They arrived at the workshop with arms full of handwritten pages of their New Testament. So as they turned to translate their Old Testament, they recruited anyone with a computer to type their New Testament. Since they had fortunately decided to use the Roman alphabet to spell their language, Westerners could keyboard for them without difficulty. What a Godsend! I first caught sight of Kris with her head down typing furiously. After a week she had become the expert in keyboarding Khawng Tu. She handed Brent and me a stack of manuscripts and said, "Get to work!" Jan took on the monumental task of collating everything.

I opened my laptop, booted up Word, and learned how to type in a language I could not speak. With multiple translators collaborating on any single book, the challenge of deciphering handwriting was significant. Initially, I wanted to ask someone to confirm about every fifth letter. Obviously, that wasn't going to work. I soon fell into a pattern of giving it my best guess. After typing, we printed proofs for the

Khawng Tu translators to spell check. After a few cycles of typing, printing, proofing, and correcting, I actually began picking up the words and patterns. Even without Khawng Tu spell-check in Word, my errors decreased and production increased. As the Khawng Tu translated their Old Testament our goal was to type, proof, correct, and print enough New Testaments so that everyone could leave with their own copy.

The MAST event coordinator, Robert Harmon, was one busy guy! In addition to answering questions and encouraging twenty-eight table leaders, he was trying to keep four printers working. In a moment of weakness, he decided to test lighter weight paper in the printers in order to reduce the thickness of the final New Testaments. The printers objected. Sometimes they would feed two pages at a time instead of just one. Printing on both sides of the page often resulted in paper jams. So as the Khawng Tu pastors lead their translation work, Robert spent an inordinate amount of time as a printer mechanic. Jan also had a lot to do, sorting through misfeeds and blanks to collate 130 New Testaments!

A Sleepless Night

Wycliffe Associates' Vice-President of Finance, Tim Neu, also participated in this workshop. But he wasn't there to manage the cash box. He was there to study the translation quality.

Before Tim became a CPA, he trained with New Tribes Mission as a church planter and Bible translator. His background meant that when MAST emerged and expanded he had a strong personal interest in the quality of the translations. Tim had been at the High Mountains MAST workshop in December 2014 and seen the tremendous results firsthand. As he and I discussed it, I encouraged him to make MAST the focus of his doctoral study and dissertation. As he researched the subject he participated in additional MAST workshops in India and wanted to include Myanmar in his study.

The Khawng Tu workshop was a bit overwhelming. With more than a hundred translators, New Testament proofing and printing, and Old Testament translation, things felt a bit chaotic to Tim. This was compounded by the fact that most of the communication was in Burmese and Khawng Tu—neither of which Tim speaks. Understandably, Tim felt like things may have gotten out of control.

He was right, and he was wrong.

His concerns kept him awake deep into the night. He realized that he was handicapped because he did not know the local languages. He asked himself, "What did I see?" He reflected on the experience of the day. He saw teams working together. One person read their Khawng Tu translation while others listened and followed along in their Burmese Bibles. Vigorous discussion followed. The pastors were involved, engaged, and leading the translations. Each team progressed at their own pace. Some seemed to have a harder time than others.

By the time morning dawned, Tim's concerns had subsided—but not disappeared. As a researcher, he decided to "trust, but verify." He sought out a translation team that was average in its composition and skill. They were working on 2 Chronicles 12. After they had completed the eight steps of MAST, Tim asked them to literally translate the Khawng Tu back into Burmese, then back into English. This took a little time, but eventually he had an oral English back-translation from the Khawng Tu. All of the narrative elements were present. All of the key theological terms were present.

One term that caught Tim's attention was the word for temple. In Myanmar there are lots of Buddhist temples. Tim wanted to know whether this was the Khawng Tu word they used for the Lord's temple. It was. Together they checked to see what Burmese word Adoniram Judson had used for temple nearly two centuries earlier. It was the Burmese equivalent for temple. The translators had done at least as well as Judson. After some discussion, everyone agreed that it was essential to include "temple of the Lord" in each reference.

Tim realized that he was not in control—God was.

Morning Devotions

Mornings always began with a time of singing, Bible study, and prayer. A couple days after I arrived I was asked to lead the Bible study for the group. As I prayed about it, I asked God to guide my heart and mind. The passage He led me to was Isaiah 55:8-11. The night before I was to lead devotions I searched out the translators who were working on Isaiah. I met an elderly man who had just translated Isaiah 55. Through an interpreter, I asked if he would be willing to read his translation in Khawng Tu for devotions. He agreed.

The next morning I invited him up front to read Isaiah 55:8-11 to the group. He held a single sheet of paper, inked and edited, limp from the humidity and sweat of his labor. He trembled as he prepared to speak. It was silent for a few moments as he gathered his courage. I stopped breathing and welled up with tears. The paper shook so hard I didn't know how he could read it. He squinted. Then he spoke. In a quiet voice, he publicly read Isaiah 55:8-11 in Khawng Tu for the first time in history.

> "For my thoughts are not your thoughts, neither are your ways my ways, declares the Lord. As the heavens are higher than the earth, so are my ways higher than your ways and my thoughts than your thoughts. As the rain and the snow come down from heaven, and do not return to it without watering the earth and making it bud and flourish, so that it yields seed for the sower and bread for the eater, so is my word that goes out from my mouth: It will not return to me empty, but will accomplish what I desire and achieve the purpose for which I sent it."

I couldn't improve on what God had said. His message was there for the Khawng Tu to hear and read for themselves—speaking into their hearts. There were moist eyes around the room. I felt obligated to say something more, so

I simply reinforced what God had said. I told the translators that the outcome of their work was guaranteed by God Himself. He said so in Isaiah 55. As His servants, we do our very best, we study, we concentrate, we pray, we use every available resource, we double-check and triple-check our work. In the end, God says His Word will accomplish the purpose for which He sent it. He. Guarantees. It.

Wrapping Up

By the end of the second week, two historic things had happened for the Khawng Tu. First, their entire New Testament was now typed, proofed, printed, and bound using a portable binding system. Every translator left with their own Khawng Tu New Testament! Second, the team of one hundred seventeen translators had managed to draft their entire Old Testament! They still had a lot of checking and keyboarding to do, but they had done a tremendous amount of translation in a very short time. The celebration was long and LOUD!

One of the Khawng Tu leaders said, "We have always been considered second class. Now we have God's Word! Now God will bless us!"

They are continuing to check their Old Testament in preparation for printing the first complete Khawng Tu Bible.

MAST is spreading virally in Myanmar. We look forward to dozens more Burmese languages translating the entire Bible.

Chapter Three

ORAL MAST

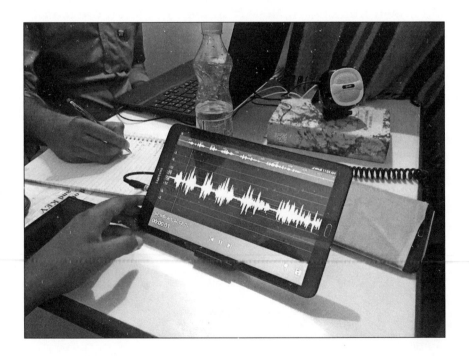

Normally we think of language as spoken communication. The reason for this is obvious. Most people
in the world communicate using spoken language. Deaf
people communicate using sign language, but that is a story
for another chapter. In our country, most of us naturally

assume that spoken languages are written. Again, the reason for this is due to our own experience.

But not everyone shares this experience.

All spoken languages are, by definition, oral. But nearly half of all spoken languages are unwritten. According to the United Nations, more than 1.2 billion people worldwide are non-literate. Tremendous efforts have been made, and are being made, to provide literacy education worldwide. Unfortunately, many minority language communities are beyond the reach of these efforts. That means literacy is a major obstacle to Bible translation.

Since Biblical times, writing has been the primary means of recording Bible translation. Scrolls, manuscripts, printing presses, typewriters, and word processors are the tools of the Bible translation trade. Alphabets and orthographies have normally been prerequisites to Bible translation. Literacy education often, understandably, precedes Scripture publication—delaying access to God's Word by years, even decades.

This was understandable when audio recordings were on wax cylinders, vinyl records, or magnetic tape. But today most of us have a digital recording device on our phones. The cost of digital memory has declined so significantly in recent years as to be essentially free today. Most of us now have print, or audio, Bibles on our phone.

But can MAST help non-literate people translate, and publish, audio Scripture in their language without intermediate written steps?

God's Preparation

Over the drone of the jet engines, Steve could hear the shriek of a missile crescendo as it raced toward its target. Unfortunately, Steve's plane was the target.

It was 1967. Steve Mercier was in Southeast Asia along with 500,000 other American troops. He was a Marine, and his plane was going down hard. Miraculously, Steve and his fellow Marines survived the crash. Their mission had taken them to the wrong side of the border, so their new objective was to make their way east—back to the official war zone.

They were vigilant for threats from every direction—on edge, physically exhausted, anxious to evade capture. They slept in shifts. About four days into their trek, Steve was shaken awake. His unit was confronted by forty locals with guns. Steve's first waking thought was of his pistol. But then he realized their guns were not aimed at him. They were merely carrying the guns for self-defense.

The Hmong people brought Steve's unit to their village, fed them, and kept them safely hidden for two months. Walking along the sand beach, breathing in the salty sea breeze, surveying the emerald mountains to the south-west and crystal clear South China Sea to the east, Steve reflected on the idyllic scene. A friend said, "I hope I never get rescued." Although the horror of war continued, God planted a tenderness for the local people in Steve's heart. God also drew Steve to Him. Some years later the Marines assigned Steve to Japan and his love for Asians expanded even more.

A New Season of Life

After returning from Asia Steve and his wife, Nancy, were living in Georgia. After the Marines Steve worked as an engineering project manager. They were involved at church, including chairing the Missions Committee. It was during these years that Steve and Nancy met a young missionary couple, Brent and Linda Ropp. The Ropps were married in that church and had been sent out as missionaries with Mission Aviation Fellowship.

When the business climate changed, Steve found himself fifty years old and out of work. So, he put his Marine training to work as a Sheriff's Deputy. A few years later the Ropps returned to visit their church and reported that they had joined Wycliffe Associates to support Bible translation. Steve heard Brent describing the lack of Scripture worldwide and the opportunities for people to use their skills and experience to advance Bible translation. Steve was intrigued but the opportunities didn't seem to fit his background. Still, Steve sent Brent his resume. Two weeks later Brent asked Steve to join our Operations team.

Steve's first job with Wycliffe Associates in 2005 was as project manager for the construction of our offices in Orlando, Florida. When that project ended, Steve and Nancy were assigned to support a key Bible translation partner—in Asia. He used his project management skills to track translation projects and budgets. They also made dear friends among the local people, and their love for Asians increased still more. In 2012 Nancy was recruited into the expanding English Language Learning (ELL) team Dan was building. Steve and Nancy moved from China to Brazil to coordinate Wycliffe Associates volunteers and facilitate ELL for our Brazilian partners. As MAST developed, and the future of ELL became less clear, Steve and Nancy returned to Orlando and had a conversation with Dan in July 2014. Dan had just returned from the first MAST workshop in the High Mountains.

Turning Back to Asia

As Steve and Nancy listened to Dan describe what had just happened in the High Mountains, they thought of the hundreds of languages without Scripture across Asia. Dan said, "We need to connect with Asian Christians who have access to minority language communities." Steve and Nancy had just lived in Asia for two years and had made many friends. Two women that had helped them with language learning immediately came to their minds. Each of them was from different minority language groups.

Since Steve and Nancy had left Asia they had lost contact with Jen and Nann.[1] They later learned that Jen had been struggling. Her business and ministry efforts were not going well. She had moved and turned off her phone and computer. For two months she fasted and prayed saying, "God, I want to serve you. But what am I going to do?" One day Jen turned her phone back on and Nann called her. "Jen. You need to answer your email. Steve wants to get in touch with you. It's important." So Jen responded to Steve's

---

[1] Pseudonyms.

email, and they began discussing the possibility of beginning Bible translation in her language.

Nann also had a friend working in evangelism and outreach in another language group. The Muxi and Lixi[2] languages include nearly 100,000 speakers but have fewer than 100 Christians. So, the plan developed to have both languages present for a MAST workshop in November 2014.

When Dan arrived, our local coordinator greeted him with, "We need to pray!" Dan quietly agreed, but the appeal escalated. "No! We really need to pray. I don't think the translators are literate!" Dan stood speechless for a moment, then the coordinator added, "I don't think these languages are written." So, they prayed. Overnight, Dan's mind was racing, thinking about the challenge of translating Scripture without reading or writing.

Oral MAST

Because these are oral cultures it seemed logical to begin by translating a Bible story. They began with the Creation story. First, they listened to an audio recording of it in the majority language. Each team then discussed the story in their own language and began to divide it into chunks for oral translation. Because everything was happening orally, the sound level was getting loud. Dan and Steve divided the teams into different rooms, then improvised using their phones to record each chunk of the oral translation. As the translators recorded successive chunks of the story, it quickly became obvious that identifying and tracking each chunk was a major challenge. In written translation, each passage connects visually with the one before and the one following. But digital audio files do not have these cues, so extra care has to go into creating and reviewing the final recording. After struggling to manage this on their phones, they purchased digital recorders locally to assist the process.

One of Jen's sisters, a church leader among the Muxi, listened to the first oral draft of the creation story. Dan asked, "What do you think?" She said, "It's accurate, but

---

2 Pseudonyms

it's not beautiful." The Muxi team agreed and used this feedback to improve their translation. This early experience in oral MAST has become part of the ongoing training for oral MAST translation in many other languages. Accuracy is essential, and beauty is part of what makes an oral translation clear and natural for the listeners.

As soon as the translation teams completed the Creation story, Dan encouraged them to begin translating Scripture. The Lixi team decided to translate Jonah. The Muxi team decided to translate Philippians.

Oral MAST uses the same eight steps as written MAST translation: consume, verbalize, chunk, blind draft, self-check, peer check, key word check, and verse-by-verse check. At each stage, revisions are made and the chunk is re-recorded until there is a final coherent recording of the passage and book. During this first oral MAST workshop, each translation team completed recording the Creation story and a single book of Scripture.

Back to the Community

Many of the people in the Muxi community received higher education in majority language universities. They were teachers, businessmen, and professionals. But the national government had instituted a program to re-educate these people. Jen's university-educated father was re-educated to become a miner. But over the years he used his education and creativity to build molds, begin a manufacturing business, and sell products made from the refined ore. Eventually, he purchased the mine using the profits from his side businesses. He also became a Christian and was excited to have the audio recording of Philippians in Muxi for the first time. He transferred the audio file from the digital recorder to his computer, and then to his cell phone. Next, he transferred the audio files to others' phones in their village.

Jen's father played the audio Scripture for one of his re-educated friends. Obviously, he had never heard it before. But from listening to the book of Philippians, this man put his faith in Jesus Christ. Read Philippians 2 for an idea of what this man heard for the first time in his life. He was soon baptized and volunteered to join the Muxi Bible translation team—putting his university education in the majority language to use translating Scriptures into Muxi.

During a family celebration, one of the translators began playing the audio recording of Philippians, and the sound overflowed into the surrounding neighborhood. The homes are close together, without solid windows or doors, so there is really no privacy. But this was actually what the translator intended. People walking through the neighborhood stopped to listen, and faith came by hearing! The whole village heard the gospel. Many people gave their lives to Christ!

Since the Muxi translators knew how to do oral MAST themselves, they began translating Psalms. The people began improvising new songs in Muxi from these translations. What started as a family celebration became a village celebration, singing songs and praising God!

The excitement in the Muxi village attracted the attention of government officials. They tracked it back to Jen and sent the police to arrest her. They also harassed her father. The police have beaten Jen multiple times, but have released her with threats of even greater harm. Jen says, "Not to worry. God is in control. I'm not afraid."

So, the Muxi and Lixi translators press on. The Muxi translators plan to complete their New Testament this year. The Lixi are translating both Old and New Testaments, and plan to complete their entire Bible by 2020.

Translation Recorder

After these early experiences with the challenges of oral MAST, it became clear that we needed better tools. Dan came back and described the challenges to Mark Stedman, our Vice-President of Information Systems. Mark put our technical team to work researching existing solutions but soon determined that these solutions were too expensive and complex for global use by local translators. A new tool would be needed.

The need for this tool coincided perfectly with another creative strategy Mark wanted to test—Five Weeks of Code.

His idea was to recruit college students studying information technology to volunteer their time and talent for five weeks during their summer break. Wycliffe Associates would provide housing, technical tools, supervision, lots of pizza, and a small stipend in exchange for their work developing a new tool to support oral MAST. Mark began promoting this idea and in a short time had a talent pool of applicants for the summer team.

During the summer of 2015, five college interns worked along with our Information Services team to create Translation Recorder (TR) from scratch. The idea was to create software that could play existing audio Bible portions in a majority language, record oral drafts and revisions in the desired minority language, and simplify the content management task needed to produce a final audio recording of the translation. All of this would be done on an inexpensive tablet computer.

Everyone involved learned a lot during this process. One thing we realized is that we needed more interns and more time. Five Weeks of Code ended with a working beta version, and we convinced one of the seniors to continue working on TR as a part-time job until he graduated in December. At that point, he joined our team to work on TR full-time.

During 2016 we field tested the beta version of TR with multiple translation teams. The concept has proven itself and we are continuing to use and develop the software based on feedback from the oral MAST events.

The Jai in India

In November of 2015, before Translation Recorder was ready to use, the Jai[3] translation team came to a MAST workshop in Northern India. The other language groups at the workshop were literate but the Jai were not. From the very start, they knew they were at a severe disadvantage. Fortunately, Steve and Nancy were part of this MAST facilitation team. Since Steve had done this before he forged ahead with his cell phone and digital recorder.

---

[3] Pseudonym

But progress was difficult. The Jai team was discouraged. As their frustration grew, it overflowed in tears. At first, Steve was uncertain how to proceed. But then he realized that they were facing spiritual warfare. Before he had understood the theory of spiritual warfare. Now he was in the midst of a battle. He enlisted Nancy to begin praying. Nancy sent the request to team members and friends back in the U.S. As prayer increased, the problems and frustrations began to decrease. The Jai persevered. Their thirst for God's Word for their people would not let them stop.

Around 130,000 people speak Jai, but there are only about 250 believers. The majority are devout Hindu, and Christians are tolerated only if they keep quiet. Satya[4] could not keep quiet. She told everyone the good news of Jesus Christ and invited them to put their faith in Him. Her husband was so angry he drove her out of their house by stoning her. She returned home to get some clothes but was again stoned by her husband and neighbors as they chased her from her village. We learned Satya's story because she was one of the Jai Bible translators.

After the November workshop, the Jai struggled with oral translation in their community. By God's grace, they were able to attend a second MAST workshop in March 2016 when TR was being field tested. They quickly learned all of the software functions. They were THRILLED with the way TR simplified and improved their work! By the end of the March workshop, they completed the oral translation of their entire New Testament!

Satya said, "I'm taking it back to my village. That means I'll get beaten again, but it's ok. I'm going anyway."

For Steve and Nancy, and for the rest of our team, this kind of courage is sobering. These believers know they will be persecuted but they will not stop. They share the gospel and the love of Christ. To them, it is more important than life. It's inspiring. It's energizing. It encourages us to continue doing everything we can to stand with these Christian brothers and sisters in their witness for Christ. Our part

---

[4] Pseudonym

seems so small compared to their sacrifice. We want to do everything we can to help them.

Multiple Oral Languages

As TR demonstrated its value, more oral MAST workshops were planned. Brent Ropp, our Vice-President of Operations, recruited his wife, Linda, and daughters, Rachel and Jennifer, to facilitate an oral MAST workshop in Rajasthan, India in July of 2016. The workshop included four unwritten languages with almost 9 million speakers. It was done in close partnership with the New Life Computer Institute (NLCI) as part of their support for Bible translation in India.

Fifty translators came to the workshop and began learning oral MAST and how to use Translation Recorder. As usual, the first couple days were trying. The translators were bilingual, in Hindi—not English. This meant that the MAST facilitation team was dependent upon just a couple English interpreters to work with a very large group. This made for a slow climb of the learning curve for the translators. Linda and Jennifer saw the frustrations firsthand. For a few days it was discouraging, but as the translators persevered they began to understand the importance of every MAST step. The English interpreters circulated to the groups that were struggling to give them extra coaching. By the end of the first week, all four teams were moving forward at an encouraging pace.

By the end of the workshop two translation teams had recorded nine books of their New Testaments, the third team recorded eleven, and the fourth team had recorded twelve!

Oral Translations

During the workshop, it was discovered that two of the four languages doing oral translations were actually written languages. So, why would they choose to do an oral translation instead of a written translation? The answer is simple—because most of their people cannot read. A written translation could have been done. They have the knowledge and capability, but most of their people would still not be able to read it for many years, if ever. By recording their oral translation first it would be immediately accessible to everyone! Now that they have their oral Bible translation they can circle back at any time to put it in writing. At this point, they don't see the need because illiteracy is so high in their communities.

As Brent worked with the language team he was facilitating, he heard a very interesting story. The people have had Scripture in Hindi for generations, and because of this they never imagined the possibility of having Scripture in their own language. They assumed that Scripture was supposed to be obscure, difficult to understand, and impersonal. They understood that Scripture said, "Go and make disciples of all nations." But they didn't understand the meaning. They knew that God spoke to people through His Word, but they didn't imagine God speaking to them in their own language.

When they considered translating Scripture into their own language they had no idea of the impact it would have on them personally. While the translation happened, they were often overwhelmed emotionally by new insights into God's Word and the realization that God was using them personally to do something with eternal impact for their people.

For them, Bible is not just history. It is now their story.

Chapter Four

CAMEROON

The first time I saw Cameroon it was from the pilot's seat of a small twin-engine airplane, flying across Central Africa toward my final destination in Kenya. It was 1992. I was serving with Mission Aviation Fellowship, delivering the plane to the base in Nairobi. Another pilot had been with me during the North Atlantic crossing, but I had dropped him off in West Africa the day before. I was all alone as I flew east.

I had been skirting the African coastline, over the Gulf of Guinea, in order to avoid the complications and financial burdens of crossing multiple national borders. Cameroon was my crossing point as I continued into Central Africa. From the north the red haze of Harmattan overflowed from the Sahara Desert, limiting my horizontal visibility. With little to see on the horizon, my gaze drifted down to the forest canopy below. The map in my hand showed a maze of rivers meandering toward the Gulf, but the dense forest below hid every river and landmark. Cameroon was a mystery slowly passing under my wings.

My Introduction to CABTAL

When I arrived at Wycliffe Associates in February 2000, I learned that we were just beginning a major construction project in Cameroon. The local Bible translation organization, the Cameroon Association for Bible Translation and Literacy (CABTAL), was formed in 1987. Wycliffe Associates was partnering with them to develop their office in the capital of Yaoundé.

This project was a key part of my early education on working in genuine partnership with the local stakeholders. Americans and Cameroonians worked side by side to build this new resource for Bible translation. The CABTAL staff impressed me from the very beginning. The faith of these men and women inspired me. As we worked to raise donations in the U.S. to cover the cost of building materials, I learned that the CABTAL staff were already financially contributing to the construction costs. Their treasure and their hearts were deeply invested in getting God's Word to every language in their nation. Their faith increased mine.

Getting More Involved

In the years following the office construction, Wycliffe Associates recruited volunteers to serve in a variety of administrative and technical support roles for CABTAL. One of our key people coordinating this support was Peg Seitz. She first went to Cameroon in 1996 as a teacher for missionary kids.

In 2006 she returned again as a teacher. But in both cases, health issues for family members cut her time in Cameroon short. In 2010 Peg moved back to Cameroon as Wycliffe Associates' Site Volunteer Coordinator. Her job was to serve CABTAL by recruiting and coordinating volunteers to assist them in their work.

Peg loved Cameroon, and she loved Cameroonians even more. She called Cameroon "the center of the universe." Her world revolved around Cameroon, and she was not shy about inviting others to serve there. Anytime she sensed that there were resources in the U.S. that could help Cameroon she worked hard to build a connection.

In 2011 Wycliffe Associates field tested new technology to provide electricity and communications to translation teams working in remote locations without reliable infrastructure. The kit consisted of a flexible solar panel, a rechargeable battery, a power controller, and a satellite communications modem. The system could be assembled and teams trained how to use it in just a half day. A short time after these were deployed in the field, the translation teams began reporting dramatic acceleration in their translation prog-ress—simply from reducing transportation and communi-cations delays. We began calling these Bible Translation Acceleration Kits (BTAKs).

The first country where we installed BTAKs was Nigeria, just west of Cameroon. Peg felt we had missed the center of the target slightly. So, within a few months, Wycliffe Associates teams installed BTAKs for eleven teams in Cameroon. Among these teams was the Weh language.

Then in early 2012, I traveled to Cameroon with three BTAKs to install and train translation teams working in the far north. Although I had been to the capital, Yaoundé, sev-eral times, this would be my first venture into the remote regions of Cameroon. I traveled with a CABTAL linguist by train, bus, and four-wheel drive to Belel, Tchouvok, and Mofu-Gudur. Working with these translation teams, in their communities, captured my heart.

I remember our arrival in the extreme northern town of Maroua, not far from the Sahara Desert. We drove across a long bridge spanning what appeared to be an ancient, dry riverbed. There was no water to be seen. But in a few spots, the people were digging, by hand or with shovels, below the dusty surface. Eventually, they would reach underground water. This is what they do to survive. For me, it became the image in my mind of the resourcefulness and perseverance of the people. They do this for water—and they do this for living water.

A New Leader

On my way to the far north, I stopped in Yaoundé to attend the twenty-fifth-anniversary celebration for CABTAL. It was a tremendous milestone, reflecting the continuing growth and health of the local commitment to Bible translation. This was also my first opportunity to meet CABTAL's new Director General, Efi Tembon.

Efi had been CABTAL's Director of Church Relations for several years and had tremendous confidence in the capacity of churches and communities to steward God's Word for their people. In their first twenty-five years, CABTAL had served twenty-four language communities. But due to a shortage of translation consultants, Efi was told not to begin any new Bible translations. At the same time, dozens of churches and communities were asking to begin! Clearly God was moving. By faith Efi agreed to support every language wanting Scripture, trusting that God would provide as only He could.

During the next three years, they grew to serve more than sixty languages as CABTAL encouraged and assisted communities to step out in faith to begin Bible translation, literacy, and community development strategies. Efi's long-term vision is to see God's Word, and community transformation, in all 279 language communities in Cameroon.

As Wycliffe Associates' English Language Learning (ELL) program expanded under Dan's leadership, naturally Peg Seitz let Efi know that this training was available to the CABTAL team. Cameroon's official languages are French and English, so some of their staff already had functional English. Others could benefit from further training to increase their access to English-language resources for Bible translation. Efi invited Dan to bring ELL to CABTAL in 2013.

The ELL training turned out to be very popular with the CABTAL staff. In fact, it turned out to be too popular. One of the elements Dan had introduced to ELL was using Skype to connect English mentors in the U.S. with international partners overseas. This enabled staff to connect online to practice their English. While this was great for English learning, it was taking time away from other Bible translation priorities in Cameroon. Efi mentioned his concern about this to Dan and me, so Dan adjusted the availability of English mentors accordingly.

When MAST was pioneered in the High Mountains in 2014, Efi was listening intently to the reports. He saw my summer Facebook post and wondered what Dan was up to. Peg was uncertain what was happening, but was anxious to see. That fall Efi traveled to the U.S. to attend a Wycliffe Associates event and had the opportunity to talk directly with Dan about the upcoming MAST workshop for the Ng people. Efi was unsure how the new MAST translation method would be received in Cameroon. Bible translation there had been following traditional translation methods for more than forty years. Most of CABTAL's translation coordinators had grown up with those methods. But Efi's experience with church and community engagement encouraged him to explore whether MAST would meet their needs.

Not in Africa

At the close of the Ng MAST workshop in the High Mountains, I was speaking with one of the translation consultants that had participated. He had more than twenty years of experience working in Bible translation in Africa. He was astonished by the work the Ng had completed using MAST and was struggling to make sense of the contrast to his prior experiences. As he searched for words he finally said, "This will never work in Africa."

I shuddered. I can't tell you how deeply this grieved my heart. His sense was that somehow the Ng were unique, that what had happened there was a miracle that could not occur in Africa. For a moment I was speechless, but my faith did not falter. God is still the God of miracles, and His sovereignty extends to Africa—and beyond.

Preparing for MAST

When Efi heard the final results from the High Mountains at the end of 2014, he asked to get Cameroon on the MAST workshop calendar. Initially, it looked as though June 2015 would be the first opportunity. Then the calendar shifted, God moved, and a slot opened for a MAST workshop in Cameroon during February.

Efi coordinated with the CABTAL team and made plans to host the MAST workshop at their training center in Bamenda. They had to reschedule other training but they didn't want to miss this early opportunity to see MAST firsthand.

Their plan was to invite three languages: one that had not started translation—Ngwo; a second that had done a small amount of translation—Tuki; and a third that was more experienced with translation—Weh. Before that plan had time to firm up, another translation team that was just getting started, Bakoko, asked to join and was accepted. The Weh team was among those we had previously connected with Bible Translation Acceleration Kits.

These four language groups include nearly 300,000 people. CABTAL invited eight translators from each language and brought twenty-one Cameroonian exegetes to serve the translation teams during the workshop. Because of the potential impact, Efi wanted to include as many of the CABTAL team as possible. He wanted to see MAST through the eyes of his colleagues and the language communities.

The Team God Invited

On the first morning of the MAST workshop, five people from the Mankon language arrived—expecting to be part of the grammar workshop that had been rescheduled. Rather than sending them away, Efi encouraged them to join the MAST workshop. Their alphabet had not been settled. Their grammar had not been studied. As they said, "When we left our homes this morning we had no idea we would be part of the translation team!"

Apparently, God had something in mind for the Mankon people.

MAST Begins

Efi welcomed everyone to the workshop and committed the time together in prayer. Dan Kramer introduced the MAST method to everyone. As Dan spoke, Efi watched the participants. Their body language was a mixture of skepticism and curiosity. Within a very short time, the CABTAL facilitators and language teams were organized. They immediately turned toward translating the book of Mark into their languages.

As the teams each began discussing Mark, voices and languages overlapped. Tentative whispers gave way to animated conversation in their mother tongues. Efi listened in as they discussed the themes and stories. He saw their body language relax. The facilitators divided Mark into the chapter assignments for individual translators. As each translator began focusing on their specific assignment the sound of turning pages and scrolling pens quieted the room.

Before lunch on the first day, Efi began hearing positive comments. CABTAL colleagues were comparing their past translation experiences to the MAST method. One of the experienced CABTAL translators applied the MAST steps to the translation he had previously done in his own language. He was shocked by the results. He said, "I need to do a revision!" The Ngwo team, who were just beginning translation, saw Scripture in Ngwo for the first time. The Mankon team, who had no idea they would be translating Scripture, improvised their alphabet and put their language—and Scripture—into writing for the first time in their history!

After lunch, the teams began checking their morning drafts: self-checking, peer-checking, key word checking, and verse-by-verse checking. As they applied the MAST method to their work they saw the clarity, naturalness, and accuracy that resulted. Enthusiasm was building. Afternoon faded into evening, but their excitement kept them working late into the night. On the first day, the teams had completed the forty-five verses of Mark 1 and were moving into chapter 2. The CABTAL exegetes were working on the verse-by-verse checks along with the translators. Efi said that lights were still on at 3 am.

The Holy Spirit was moving, and the translation teams were moving with Him!

The Weekend

The Mankon team was ecstatic! Folera described his translation partner Kien, "Her spirit is in heaven now! She is writing in Mankon!" Kien was one of the teachers that had come expecting to study Mankon grammar. But God had other plans! The Mankon team sent word back to their community about what was happening. Their families and friends were shocked! Kien contacted her pastor and asked whether she could read the first chapter of Mark in Mankon on Sunday. He agreed.

A few of our Wycliffe Associates team traveled to Ntanka Presbyterian Church with Kien that weekend. During the service, the pastor invited the Mankon translation team to report on the MAST workshop and the progress they were making in translating Scripture into Mankon. In the congregation, hearts were overflowing with thanksgiving. Though they were some of the first Christians in the region, they had seen many other language groups around them get Scripture translations before them. They had been waiting a long time. They felt like they were the last to get the Scriptures in their language—but the day they had long prayed for had arrived! God was using Mankon Christians to translate His Word for their own community!

That morning Pastor Franklin changed his sermon. After hearing Mark 1 in Mankon, he preached from verses 9-13, on Jesus's baptism.

The Results

By the end of the second week of the workshop all five language groups had completed the book of Mark. The Ngwo team went beyond Mark and began translating I Thessalonians. Men and women who had never translated before realized that God had prepared them as only He could to do this work for their people. Experienced Cameroonian translators, some who were skeptics just days before, could not imagine going back to the translation methods they had previously used.

On the last day, the teams celebrated the work that God had done in and through them. After a time of prayer and singing, printed copies of the book of Mark were given to each of the translators in their own language.

One of the older Bakoko men stood to speak. "We thought it would take ten years to complete our New Testament," he said, "and I don't think I will be here in ten years. But now we see it can be done in just a few years. I can still be here then!"

By God's grace, Peg Seitz was able to be present in Cameroon for this MAST workshop. God gave her a glimpse at the future of Bible translation in Cameroon. It turned out to be her final overseas trip before God called her home to heaven.

Everyone involved in Bible translation is committed to translating Scripture accurately. This was one of the biggest questions for CABTAL surrounding MAST. What they found was that the quality of the translation is better than before. The checking of accuracy is rigorous and immediate. The translations are clearer and more natural. Their experienced translation consultants have more confidence in the accuracy of the translations because of the strong engagement of the local church in each language group.

When the Ngwo team returned to their community their Nge neighbors heard what they had done and asked them to teach them the MAST method. The Mogamo community also learned MAST from their neighbors. MAST began spreading virally in Cameroon!

The Mystery is Broken

There is a Cameroonian proverb that says, "One hand cannot tie a bundle." The churches saw that MAST gave them what they were previously missing in order to do Bible translation themselves.

Henri, another of the Bakoko translators said, "This is indeed surprising that translations can be as fast as these. We have spent a lot of time translating only a small portion of the Scripture before this method was introduced to us. But from now, I think translation is no longer a **mystery** and a stressful task. We shall speed the translation using this method since the churches desperately need Scripture. We thank God who used our brothers and sisters from the West to extend this knowledge to us."

Kien said, "I thought from the beginning I will not be able to translate even a word as I was asked to attend the grammar workshop. But I found myself doing translation with all ease and joy! When I look at the translation I have done after the checks, I begin to ask myself whether I am the one who has done this great task. The **mystery** is broken!"

CABTAL exegete, Rev. Ngole David, said, "When this method was introduced I had to ask Dan many questions, only to find out whether this was going to be a success and how feasible will this be. But when I started doing a verse-by-verse check with the Mankon team that is when I realized that this is real business, and this whole **mystery** of Bible translation is broken at last. We took ten years to translate our New Testament. If this method was introduced to us we would have finished in three years to meet the aspirations and high demand for Scripture in the Bakossi land. We hope this will be extended to other language teams so that the demands of the mother tongue Scripture will be met without unnecessary delays and bottlenecks. I think we had a great problem, and at last we have found a solution."

Efi Tembon says, "MAST **demystifies** Bible translation. For too long Bible translation has been a secret held by foreigners. No more. Changing to MAST has required changes to our organizational culture. But God is using

CABTAL to serve His church as they steward His Word in each language."

CABTAL's Plan

CABTAL held their second MAST workshop in June of 2015. Soon after this workshop, Efi gathered the CABTAL team together to discuss how to best integrate MAST into their holistic work with language communities. MAST did not arrive in Cameroon in a vacuum. A widespread community transformation movement was already well underway. In order for MAST to serve the Cameroonian communities, it had to be contextualized. It had to become Cameroonian, and that is exactly what happened.

CABTAL has transitioned all of their translation projects to use MAST. They have grown from sixty Bible translation projects to more than eighty. All of their Biblical exegetes have become MAST facilitators. Their plan is to hold twelve MAST workshops in Cameroon each year—four in Yaoundé, four in Bamenda, and four in Maroua. They are not dependent on Wycliffe Associates. They are leading MAST themselves. It is their strategy.

Most of the Bible translations using MAST in Cameroon are in languages that have an alphabet. But the challenge of translating unwritten languages is significant. Imposing literacy requirements adds years of delays before oral communities can translate Scripture. Wycliffe Associates' new tool, Translation Recorder, is enabling non-literate communities to create audio translations from audio Bibles without intermediate written steps. CABTAL is learning how to put these tools to work for the oral language communities of Cameroon.

The challenge of sign language Bible translation is even more daunting. It is estimated that there are more than four hundred unique sign languages throughout the world. In July of 2016, CABTAL held their first sign language MAST workshop in Cameroon for two sign languages. Churches invited thirty deaf members to review and check the initial videos. Because they are generally isolated from the hearing community, it is important to build the ownership of Bible translation within this community. CABTAL docs not want sign language translation to be dependent on their organization. They want the deaf community to have all of the resources they need to steward God's Word themselves.

There are still more than fifty languages in Cameroon without any Scripture. CABTAL believes that MAST will enable all of these languages to have God's Word within a few years.

Beyond Cameroon

After CABTAL demonstrated the value of MAST in Africa, other Bible translation partners began contacting them to learn more. CABTAL has invited translation partners from across Africa and Asia to attend MAST workshops in Cameroon and learn from their experiences.

In recent years church leaders from Gabon, just south of Cameroon, contacted CABTAL asking for assistance in forming a similar Bible translation organization in their country. Efi traveled to Libreville in 2015 to explain to Gabonese church leaders that they could accomplish Bible translation themselves using MAST. After Efi met with church leaders from multiple Christian denominations, the churches decided to host their first MAST workshop in July 2016. CABTAL's MAST facilitators led the workshop for seven Gabonese languages. They also invited Dan to facilitate their first effort to use MAST for translating Scripture into sign language for the deaf community. Gabon has at least thirty languages that are still without Scripture, but now they have the means to accomplish these translations themselves. Naturally, CABTAL is ready and willing to help their neighbors.

Chapter Five

THE SUBCONTINENT

Through most of history, India has been shrouded in mystery for the Western world. That began to change during the European Age of Discovery. When explorers arrived, they found that India was highly advanced in both arts and sciences and had a deep cultural and religious heritage in Hinduism.

In 1600 the British East India Company was chartered to develop and manage British trade with India. Initially,

British trade increased steadily and peaceably. The decline of Mughal political power, and trade competition from the French East India Company, eventually led to armed confrontations to protect British trade interests. These escalated to the point where private company armies were battling for control of large geographic areas of India. The British East India Company armies ultimately prevailed and effectively ruled India from 1757 to 1858. At that time increasing Indian rebellion led to the British government disbanding the company and assuming direct control of Indian government. This continued until the growing Indian civil disobedience movement under Mohandas (Mahatma) Gandhi succeeded in gaining independence for India in 1947.

William Carey

William Carey has been described by many as the father of modern missions. Born in England in 1761, he grew up in the Church of England. During his school years, he found that he had both interest and gifting in learning foreign languages. He taught himself Latin, Greek, and Hebrew. In his teen years, he became discontent with the Church of England, joining other dissenters to form a Congregational church. After school, he apprenticed as a shoemaker and taught himself Italian, Dutch, and French in his spare time. At the age of twenty, he married Dorothy and they began a family.

Not long after marrying, Carey joined a small group affiliated with the Particular Baptist denomination. He was baptized and invited to preach in their church every other Sunday. At the age of twenty-four, he was asked to pastor the church. During his years as a pastor, he was influenced by the writings and biographies of international explorers and Puritan missionaries. This led to his own theological and missiological reflections on the place of international missionary efforts. In 1792 he published his book *An Enquiry into the Obligations of Christians to Use Means for the Conversion of the Heathens*. The immediate result of this book was the formation of the Baptist Missionary Society. One of their first missionaries was a medical doctor working in Calcutta. The next year the Carey family accompanied him to India.

Carey immediately began learning the Bengali language. He took a job as manager of an indigo processing plant to support his family. Within six years he had completed the translation of the New Testament into Bengali. His language skills and interest led him to study ancient Sanskrit and translate the epic poem *Ramayana* into English. During the remaining years of his ministry in India, he translated the full Bible into Bengali, Sanskrit, Oriya, Marathi, Hindi, and Assamese. He also translated portions of the Bible into several other Indian languages and dialects.

My Introduction

In 2001 I attended my first international conference of Bible translation leaders. I sat in the audience surrounded by more than four hundred international leaders in Bible translation. During the plenary sessions, I began to hear experienced perspectives on the global opportunities and challenges facing Bible translation. I was on a steep learning curve with just over one year serving in Wycliffe Associates. Every presentation and conversation was an opportunity for me to add depth and breadth to my understanding of how we would best serve Bible translation.

Sixteen years later only one conversation I had at that conference remains vivid in my memory. In one of the large group sessions, an Indian leader was invited to the platform to formally recognize their organizational partnership in Bible translation. His name is Jacob George Chavanickamannil, but we call him Jacob George. During the break following his recognition, I sought him out to introduce myself and learn more about Bible translation in India. It was a part of the world about which I knew very little. That conversation was the beginning of a deep and enduring friendship and partnership in ministry.

Indian Bible Translators

In the coming years, Jacob began to describe his vision for training Indian Christians to translate Scripture into their own languages. He saw their language and cultural diversity as part of God's preparation for every language in India to have His Word. Their primary limitation was a small rented facility that was inadequate for the scale of training they envisioned. I joined Jacob in praying for God's wisdom in how this vision might become reality. It soon became clear that Wycliffe Associates was part of the answer to these prayers.

Since our formation in 1967 Wycliffe Associates has provided design and construction assistance for partners in Bible translation worldwide. We engage Christian professionals from these specialties in volunteer service opportunities. We've built and repaired homes, offices, schools, airstrips—and dozens of training centers for national translators. The scale of the need for Scripture translation in India suggested that developing this facility would stretch our faith and resources.

I traveled to India in 2007 to meet Jacob's colleagues and visit a potential location for the training center. Because many of the remaining translation needs were in the northern tier of Indian states, a plan was developed to partner with a Christian seminary there to offer Bible translation training as part of their pastoral church-planting curriculum.

The seminary had undeveloped land they offered to make available for construction of faculty residences, offices, classrooms, and a student dormitory. They saw Bible translation as a natural extension and complement to their existing seminary classes. The essence of a collaborative agreement was already worked out before I joined the conversation. I was encouraged by the plans and agreed that Wycliffe Associates would provide design and construction supervision to develop the necessary facilities.

Once the site was chosen our architectural and engineering team began creating designs that reflected the vision. We asked one of our experienced Construction Superintendents if he would be willing to supervise the multi-year development. Dave and Sandy Jackson moved to India to manage the project with the local Indian contractors.

In February of 2012, the first phase of the Wycliffe India Institute of Languages and Linguistics was completed. This phase included faculty residences, offices, and class-rooms. Students began training in Bible translation the next semester. It was soon obvious that the level of student interest would exceed the capacity of existing student dor-mitories. The second phase of dormitory construction was completed in November 2015.

Among the first occupants of the dormitory that month were translators from the Khirwar and Jai language com-munities, along with our facilitation team, as they began New Testament translations using MAST.

MAST Begins in India

The introduction of MAST to India was in December 2014, immediately following the MAST workshop where the Ng translators completed half of their New Testament in two weeks. Dan was invited to describe MAST to a net-work of Indian ministry partners called the Last Command Initiative (LCI). These ministries work together in an effort to assure that every language and ethnic group in India has a sustainable Christian witness. They do evangelism, church planting, discipleship, leadership training, and Bible trans-lation to support these goals. At that time they had identi-fied 110 languages in India that were without a single verse of Scripture.

Following the life-changing experience with the Ng trans-lation team, Dan was excited to share what God had just accomplished. The LCI meeting had a busy agenda but they set aside two sessions for our Wycliffe Associates team to present the MAST translation methodology. Dan reported the results from the three workshops that had previously taken place and updated them regarding the information technology tools and resources that we were developing to support Bible translation work. He described the origin of MAST and how it had developed over the previous year. Then he described the eight steps of MAST in detail, highlighting the authority and engagement of the local church, and church responsibility for quality control. All of these church leaders had experience with Bible translation under foreign control. They were interested to hear that MAST relies on local church involvement and were encouraged by the results that other Asian churches had using MAST.

One of the other tools that the Wycliffe Associates team described at the LCI meeting was Open Bible Stories. This is a collection of twenty-one Old Testament and twenty-nine New Testament stories released under Creative Commons licensing. This allows anyone to use the illustrations and translate the stories into any language without further permission or paying royalties. Three aspects of Open Bible Stories were of immediate interest to the Indian church leaders. First, telling stories is a common way for Indians to communicate wisdom and teaching in their communities. Introducing these Bible stories would be a natural fit for their existing evangelism and discipleship strategies. Second, translating the stories would require much less time than translating full books of the Bible. It seemed like a natural starting point to test the MAST translation method and see the results. Third, the Old Testament stories would add Old Testament history and context in places where the primary teaching had been from the New Testament.

After hearing Dan's description of MAST, all seven LCI partner organizations asked to test MAST in their ministries. Some wanted to immediately begin translating the Open Bible Stories. Others were anxious to test Scripture translation. The prospect of engaging their churches and having Scripture in their languages within just a couple years moved them to action.

Momentum Builds

Three LCI partners brought translation teams from eighteen languages to the first Indian MAST event in March 2015 in Hosur, in southern India. Their goal was to translate Open Bible Stories. Mike Hatfield, Dan's former pastor, led the event. At the time, this was the largest gathering of languages and translators ever for a MAST event. More than fifty translators participated. Facilitating a group this large proved to be a good experience for our MAST team, as it was an indication of things to come in India.

A fourth LCI partner organized the next MAST event in May 2015 to begin translating the New Testament into a language of northeastern India. This is a people group of 194,000 speakers with just a few dozen Christians. As a result, the translation team included a mixture of believers and unbelievers from the community. Initially, this was a major concern for the MAST facilitators. As the workshop unfolded it became clear that the language skills of the unbelievers were contributing significantly to the quality of the translation. The believers also saw this as a unique opportunity to teach God's Word to the unbelievers. By the end of the two-week workshop they had completed seven New Testament books, and the team was motivated to continue to complete their New Testament in their communities.

Within the first year, all seven LCI partners had participated in a MAST workshop. As mentioned previously, Wycliffe India hosted a MAST event at their Institute for Languages and Linguistics in northern India in November 2015. They invited translators from the Khirwar and Jai languages. There are 34,000 Khirwar speakers and 130,000 Jai speakers. During the two-week workshop, the Khirwar team translated seventeen New Testament books—seven more than they had planned!

The Jai had the additional challenge of not being a written language, but some of our facilitators had already tackled the challenge of oral translation by this time. So the Jai had a pathway to follow as they worked.[5] After the encouraging progress made in their first workshop, the Khirwar and Jai teams returned in March 2016 to finish translating their New Testaments.

---

[5] A more detailed description of the Jai translation is given in the chapter titled Oral MAST.

A New Partner in India

While the translation events were underway in India during November 2015, I was invited to attend the annual conference of the Biblical Institute for Leadership Development (BILD) in Ames, Iowa. Members of our Wycliffe Associates team had connected with BILD leaders in the years prior as we overlapped with their leadership development ministry in several locations around the world. BILD asked us to assist them in translating their leadership training curriculum from English into other major languages around the world, including Hindi. As we assisted them in this effort we learned that the BILD student network included more than 400,000 Christian leaders worldwide! Previous discussion with BILD leaders surfaced the possibility of developing a Bible translation track as part of their accredited Masters and Doctoral degree programs. In the months before this conference, our teams had worked hard to create this Bible translation track. The gathering in Iowa brought a few hundred of these international leaders together for several days of training, worship, fellowship, and networking.

My Wycliffe Associates colleagues had already introduced MAST to the group before I arrived. Although Bible translation was not a high priority on the agenda for that meeting, the buzz about MAST was tangible by the time I arrived. When I was invited to speak to the group, I reminded them that it had been nearly five hundred years since the Reformation opened the door for Bible translation into every language—and I challenged them to launch this Reformation in their own languages. When we passed around a sign-up sheet for the leaders to indicate their interest in beginning Bible translation in their languages—two hundred and nine leaders signed up! These included African, Asian, South American, and India leaders. Because of BILD's strong network in India, this became the natural place for BILD to launch their Bible translation degree program.

BILD's first MAST workshops were in Eastern India in January 2016. That month they launched new translations in eight languages. That February they started new Bible translations in thirty-nine languages. By the end of 2016

BILD students had begun Bible translation in seventy-three languages in India!

Spiritual Warfare

Some Hindus claim there are 330 million gods, and there are one billion Hindus in India. There are also 172 million Muslims in India. This adds up to a lot of opposition to Christians, and Christian ministries. Right now India ranks fifteenth on Open Doors' World Watch List for Christian persecution. Clearly, this is a challenging context for Bible translation.

From the progress already described, it may seem like MAST expanded in India without any challenges. That is definitely not the case. The progress of Bible translation in India is the result of the movement of the Holy Spirit—doing things only God can do. Indian church leaders cast a vision for God's Word in every language and recruited believers to form translation teams. Hundreds of Indian Christians responded to these invitations with courage and commitment. Extraordinary collaboration across denominational lines and ethnic boundaries has characterized this movement. None of this has escaped Satan's attention. He battles for every soul.

Initially, we noticed logistical challenges, visa problems, and scheduling conflicts regularly challenging us. It was easy to write these off as the routine difficulties of working internationally. Then people started getting ill at the MAST events—not just one or two, but dozens. It wasn't just the foreign MAST facilitators. That could have been explained by the normal challenges of dietary differences. The local translators were also getting sick, but the thirst for God's Word was so great that none of this deterred the work.

MAST faced other early challenges from a few translators who were experienced in other translation methods. This has been common in many places where some translation has occurred. In India this surfaced with questions about the MAST method, objections to decisions made by the MAST facilitators, criticism of the local translators, and demands for additional training and resources. At one event a foreign translator collected the first drafts by the local translators before they had gone through the four quality checking steps and criticized the quality prematurely. Some of the Indian translators complained that their long-term employment as translators would likely be at risk because the MAST progress was too quick. While none of this is indisputably spiritual warfare, the confusion and contention it produced along the way were clear evidence of Satan's attempts to oppose progress in Bible translation.

At another event our MAST facilitator, Joe Gervais, was awakened by his Indian roommate who described a vivid dream he had just had. In the dream, Joe told his roommate to turn around. When he turned, he saw that there was a cobra behind him. Neither Joe nor his roommate knew what to make of the dream—but they immediately prayed together for a hedge of protection for everyone at the workshop. During the first part of the day things proceeded normally, but late that morning Joe was told that one of the women translators and her nephew had to leave the workshop because her brother, the nephew's father, had died during the previous night. His father had been bitten by a snake. Naturally, this caused concern for this translation team. They gathered around the woman and her nephew to pray for them as they departed. Later that evening a MAST facilitator who had been working with another translation team casually commented to Joe about an unusual experience during the day. As he walked past the affected translation team's table the image of a cobra striking a man in a field came to mind. The next day the lead pastor of that language team reported that the father had been bitten by a cobra.

Joe said, "I don't find it coincidental that my roommate and another member of our MAST team had independent visions and specific images of the cobra, and that it was indeed a cobra that killed the brother of one of the translators. We'd been praying, and hundreds of partners around the world were praying for a hedge of protection for us and the translators at the workshop. Unfortunately, Satan was able to find a weakness in the hedge of protection with a family member and use that to battle the progress of translating God's Word for these people."

Other translators describe the severe persecution that they face within their language community. Many have been beaten. Some have had their children kidnapped—not for money, but to coerce the Christians to denounce their faith publicly. Others have been evicted from their homes, driven out of their communities by stoning, and lived in severe physical deprivation. Yet, for every one of these stories there is a testimony of God's miraculous intervention through healing, protection, or unexpected provision for their needs. The believers smile and praise God for His love and salvation. They are humbled that He invited them to share in getting His Word to their family, friends, and enemies.

The spiritual battle continues.

As in Acts

At the December 2015 LCI meeting, these partners had identified 110 Indian languages without Scripture. During the next eighteen months, Bible translation began in ninety-one languages. Plans are developing now to launch, and complete, Bible translations in every remaining Indian language without Scripture.

How is any of this possible?

William Carey did not attend seminary. He did not receive formal language training. He learned Biblical and foreign languages by studying them himself. His contemporaries described his mastery of English grammar and spelling as poor. Yet he translated the Bible into six Indian languages—all while holding down jobs, overcoming challenges, and involving himself in benevolent efforts for the communities in which he lived.

Many of the Indian translators today are much more highly qualified to do Bible translation than Carey was. Many have attended university or seminary. All of them grew up multi-lingual. They have known their own language for a lifetime—not merely studying it for a few years. They understand their own culture thoroughly as insiders. They are members and leaders in their churches, networked with hundreds of other believers for counsel and perspective.

The most obvious gift that all of these Indian translators, and William Carey, share is the gift of tongues—not in the sense of speaking unintelligible spiritual languages, but in the sense of extraordinary gifting in languages that are understood broadly. This reminds me of Acts 2 when people from around the world heard the disciples "declaring the wonders of God" in their own languages.

The other gift that all of these translators share is the gift of the Holy Spirit. Jesus said, "But you will receive power when the Holy Spirit comes upon you; and you will be my witnesses in Jerusalem, and in all Judea and Samaria, and to the ends of the earth." Does the Holy Spirit that inspired the writers of Scripture still have the power to guide the pens and computers of Bible translators today? Is Bible translation part of God's plan for His testimony to be known by every nation, tribe, people, and language?

Indian Christians would emphatically answer, "Yes!" Our opportunity is to serve and support them in their translation work.

Chapter Six

ETHIOPIA

E thiopia is an ancient center of mankind and civilization
by every measure. Prehistoric archeological discoveries
confirm human settlements among the earliest dates. The
Genesis account describes the descendants of Noah's son,
Ham, and Ham's eldest son, Cush, who settled in the region

surrounding the Red Sea and throughout the Horn of Africa. Three centuries before Christ, the Septuagint translation translated the Hebrew "Kush" as "Aithiopia." The subsequent historical record confirms the continuity of Ethiopia through the present day. It is the oldest independent nation in Africa. It is also the second largest African nation in population, with more than one hundred million people.

Early Bible Translation

The Acts 8 account of Philip witnessing to the Ethiopian government treasury official is a first-century description of Christian testimony impacting a person of influence and authority in Ethiopia. Depending on various historical perspectives, Ethiopia is either the first or second (following Armenia) nation to declare itself Christian. It is certainly the first African nation to do so.

By the fourth century AD, the Bible had been translated into the ancient Ethiopian language of Ge'ez. For centuries this has been the Biblical and liturgical text for the Orthodox Christian Church in Ethiopia.

But Ge'ez is an extinct language. It is no longer in common usage.

The Amharic Bible

The first Amharic Bible translation manuscript dates back to the early nineteenth century, by an Ethiopian named Abu Rumi. The complete Bible translation was not published in print until 1840.

Early in the reign of Emperor Haile Selassie I, a modern Amharic translation was completed. When Italy invaded Ethiopia during World War II this translation was sent to England for printing. However, most of the printed copies were destroyed by fire during bombing in London. This same translation was printed with funding from the United States, but most copies were later destroyed after serious translation errors were discovered.

In 1962 another modern Amharic Bible translation from original Hebrew and Greek texts was completed by a committee chartered by the Emperor. This translation was updated by the Ethiopian Orthodox Church in 1986.

While Amharic is the official national language of Ethiopia, it is worth noting that only about 17% of the population speak Amharic as their first language. Amharic as a second language is spoken by only another 4% of the population. Said another way, only about one in four Ethiopians understand Amharic.

Recent Years

There are more than eighty languages spoken throughout Ethiopia. During the late twentieth century, Western linguistic researchers studied and documented about thirty of these languages. Ethiopian linguists, academics, researchers, and literacy specialists contributed extensively to these language development efforts. Ethiopian Bible translators also translated portions of the Bible into more than twenty languages, but the overall progress of Bible translation has not kept pace with the growth of the Christian church in Ethiopia and has not yet reached tens of millions of Ethiopians.

The desire for Scripture in local languages has been growing within Ethiopian churches for years. Christian churches increasingly recognize that evangelism, church planting, and discipleship depend on access to Scripture in a language and form that the local people understand. The vision for an Ethiopian Bible translation organization grew, then came to fruition with the formation of Wycliffe Ethiopia in 2013.

An Ethiopian Leader

God had been preparing Tefera Endalew to lead a new season of Ethiopian Bible translation for many years. After graduating from college, Tefera began teaching at a Bible school. This gave him the full-time opportunity to study and teach the Bible. In 1999 he began coordinating literacy for seventy-two churches affiliated with the largest evangelical Christian denomination in Ethiopia. Tefera also began serving as a church pastor within the Me'en language community. In 2005 he earned a Bachelor of Theology in Translation and Linguistics. In the years following he became the Multi-Lingual Education Coordinator for six language groups, touching 700,000 speakers and leading a team of thirty-nine colleagues.

When Wycliffe Ethiopia officially formed in 2013 Tefera was invited to be the founding Executive Director. The next year he completed his Master's Degree in Literacy from Gloucester University in the U.K.

Initial Evaluation

Tefera's first priority in launching Wycliffe Ethiopia was to recruit a team of experienced colleagues, many of whom had worked in linguistic development efforts during the prior decades. Within just a few months of formation, Tefera heard about the emergence of a new church-centered Bible translation method called MAST. He soon contacted Dan Kramer to learn more about the academic and philosophical foundations of MAST. Tefera wanted to evaluate the foundation of MAST based on his background in linguistics, literacy, and multi-lingual education. After receiving Dan's academic papers, Tefera gathered the Wycliffe Ethiopia team and other international Bible translators to study and prayerfully evaluate the potential for MAST in Ethiopia. These discussions generated a number of questions that Tefera sent back to Dan for response, but the Ethiopians' were encouraged by several of the fundamental premises of MAST.

One aspect of MAST that immediately resonated with them was that Bible translation is the work of the Church. Twenty centuries of Christian history in Ethiopia show that the Church is ready, willing, and able to steward this responsibility. Also, because MAST engages the people and resources already within the local church there is no need to wait for foreign resources before starting. There is no need to delay. Bible translation can begin immediately.

The second element of MAST that encouraged the Ethiopians was that it reflected their own sense of urgency. One of the Wycliffe Ethiopia team members had previously worked with a New Testament translation that was in process for thirty years and was still not finished. Tefera had worked with another New Testament translation that was still incomplete after thirty-two years of work. The prospect of starting, and finishing, a New Testament translation in mere months increased the anticipation of the Wycliffe Ethiopia team. In their own words, "We should not take a century." "Christ is coming. We need to do this now!" "People are hungry for the Word of God!" "People do not want to wait a long time. This is what I love about MAST!"

As the team evaluated the key translation and quality checking steps of MAST, they recognized that it includes all of the elements of traditional translation models. The presence of these familiar steps gave them faith that the translation would be accurate. Everyone involved in Bible translation understands, indeed strives for, a translation that faithfully reflects the original Biblical texts. A poor translation serves no one. So, while MAST adds several innovations to Bible translation, it builds on the foundation of translation principles proven over decades of work.

After days of discussion, evaluation, reflection, and prayer, the Wycliffe Ethiopia team had a deep sense of God's hand at work. They decided to put MAST to work in Ethiopia in 2015.

Getting Started

Because of the importance of story-telling in Ethiopian cultures, the decision was made to use the MAST method to accelerate the translation of Bible stories. Open Bible Stories is an open-license Biblical resource that includes twenty-one Old Testament, and twenty-nine New Testament, stories. Since it is open-license it can immediately be translated into any language without further permission or payment of royalties. Wycliffe Ethiopia's goal is to translate these fifty Bible stories into all eighty-seven languages in Ethiopia.

As they applied the MAST methods to the translation of these Bible stories, they also began preparations to put MAST to work in New Testament translations. As Tefera developed this plan with the Wycliffe Ethiopia team, they expanded the discussion to include Ethiopian church leaders and other African leaders in Bible translation. As the enthusiasm for the potential impact within Ethiopia continued to rise, others outside Ethiopia voiced concern and urged caution in exploring MAST.

As Tefera listened to the counsel and concerns he felt that the best way to respond would be to create an open test of MAST, inviting everyone that was interested to participate and see it firsthand. The invitation went out to all of Wycliffe Ethiopia's partners. As the responses came back it became clear that Wycliffe Ethiopia had touched a sensitive nerve. The responses fell into three general categories. Ethiopian church leaders enthusiastically agreed to participate. Some of Wycliffe Ethiopia's international partners responded more cautiously, choosing not to participate in the MAST translations, but agreeing to send people to observe and evaluate it. Others declined to participate in any way.

The Languages

The time for the MAST Bible translation workshop was set for August 2015. As the planning proceeded the Wycliffe Ethiopia team wanted to be sure that the language groups included would reflect a mix of church denominations and local Bible translation partners.

The Ethiopian Kale Heywet Church (EKHC) is the largest evangelical Christian denomination in Ethiopia, with more than 7,000 congregations and over 8.5 million members. Leaders from the EKHC were closely involved in the formation of Wycliffe Ethiopia and were enthusiastic about the potential for MAST in Ethiopia. They invited the Dime language, from southwestern Ethiopia, to participate in the MAST test.

One of the international partners invited the Baiso and Gayil people to participate. Wycliffe Ethiopia invited the Inor and Ch'ara people to participate.

Together these five languages include around 393,000 people without one verse of Scripture. All of these languages are located in southwestern Ethiopia, so the decision was made to hold the MAST workshop in Awassa, 175 miles south of the capital of Addis Ababa.

The Workshop Begins

Around sixty people gathered in Awassa for the MAST workshop. Just over half of the group were translators. Wycliffe Ethiopia and partner facilitators, Wycliffe Associates MAST leaders, and international observers comprised the rest of the group. Day one opened with prayer, greetings, organization of the translation teams, and the introduction of MAST to the entire group. English instructions were first interpreted in Amharic and then discussed in each of the five languages.

By noon on the first day, translation began with a mixture of fear and excitement. As each team worked, unique qualities and challenges became apparent.

The Dime translation team included three church leaders, a Bible school teacher, a youth minister, and two women's ministry leaders. But three-quarters of all the Dime people are monolingual, and their literacy rate is less than one-percent, so their team understood less Amharic than the other groups. The Ch'ara translators were also not literate. This meant they had to spend much more time than other groups on the very first MAST step—consuming the text. The Ethiopian facilitators for these groups spoke neighboring languages, so extra time was taken to build the Dime and Ch'ara teams' understanding of each passage. The additional discussion helped them to think critically and internalize the verses before they began translating.

The Gayil team included six men. One had two years of theology training, while all of the others had a twelfth-grade education. Their knowledge of Amharic and their literacy was good. So by the end of Monday afternoon they had already drafted several chapters. For this group, the MAST steps seemed like a good way to study the Bible in depth. At first, they struggled with blind drafting but soon recognized how natural their translation sounded. As they began peer checking they were uncomfortable questioning one another's work, but they gained confidence as they saw the benefit. When they ran into difficult passages the facilitator would have them translate from Gayil back into Amharic so they could check to be sure nothing was added or missed. They had vigorous discussions to be sure they were all using the same key-terms for theological accuracy.

The Baiso and Inor teams were passionate and engaged quickly. Inor is a large people group with nearly 300,000 speakers and 128,000 Christians. The Baiso population is under 8,000 but eighty-eight percent are Christians. Both of these teams reflected the deep thirst of their people for God's Word.

Reflecting on MAST in Process

As the translators worked the Ethiopian facilitators observed, encouraged, and reflected on how MAST compared to their prior experience in Bible translation.

Seeing the translators begin translation on the first day, with minimal training, was disconcerting. Most of the facilitators had spent months in training before ever beginning translation. It was also awkward for the most experienced translators to be observing the least experienced translators working. It felt backward and uncomfortable.

Each translation team, and even each translator, moved at their own pace. Because some teams were literate and others were not, some worked quietly while others were constantly talking. Translators were using a variety of source texts. Most were in Amharic, but even these included different versions. Some had English or other Ethiopian language translations nearby. Some teams were more educated than others. The sheer number of variations seemed chaotic and disorganized. Translators and facilitators felt confused. Complaints surfaced.

In the midst of all this, Dan was noticeably calm. He had seen and heard all of this before while leading MAST workshops in other countries. While MAST includes all of the key elements of traditional translation methods, implementing them simultaneously with larger translation teams is unconventional. Dan reassured the facilitators and the translators. "Trust the process. Don't skip uncomfortable steps. Every step is important. Give it a try. You can do it!"

The frustration of day one dissolved as the translation teams gained experience with the eight steps of MAST. By day two each team had found their own balance and pace. They were encouraged to see verse after verse, passage after passage, chapter after chapter building and connecting. They were seeing God's Word come to life in their own language after generations of silence. What was previously cloaked in darkness, became bright in their eyes and hearts. By day three MAST was their method of Bible translation.

The translators liked the simplicity of the MAST method. They were amazed and excited by their progress. They saw the naturalness and clarity of the translation. They checked the accuracy of their translations against the source texts and saw the quality of their work. "This sounds good!"

The Ethiopian facilitators also gained confidence. What they had read in Dan's theory papers was coming true before their very eyes. Their questions were answered. "It was amazing! They did it! This is very good work!"

External Perspective

As the Ethiopians worked, the international observers observed. Comparisons and contrasts to traditional translation methods were recorded. At the end of the workshop, they produced a nineteen-page evaluation of MAST from their perspective.

Their concerns regarding MAST generally fell into two categories.

First, they were concerned regarding the qualifications of the translators. None had linguistic degrees. None had previously done any Bible translation. Translation training was minimal. Some were not literate. They did their work with paper and pen, or in the case of the Dime with a recorder, without the aid of computers. In short, the translators did not meet external expectations.

Second, the observers were concerned that the translations would not be under the authority of established Bible translation agencies.

It is important to note that no one at the workshop raised any concerns regarding the MAST method itself. No one criticized the eight steps of MAST. No one pointed to evidence of errors in the translations. The concerns all focused on the implementation and management of the process.

Local Perspective

One of the realities often faced in cross-cultural situations is that internal and external values and perspectives are different. This is, in fact, why cultures are different. The translators involved were selected by their church leaders. They were chosen based on their knowledge of their language and culture, their Christian faith, and their testimony in their community. They were chosen based on the judgment and values of the local church.

The primary experience that these language communities had with established Bible translation agencies was that they were overlooked. While other surrounding languages were studied and translated, theirs were not. They were told to wait, or worse yet—that their language had been determined not to need translation. Translation efforts were not established in their communities. However, the church has been established for centuries. The church is the recognized authority for Scripture in these communities.

In Their Own Words

When describing the beginning of Bible translation in his heart language, one man responded with an Ethiopian proverb. "When mom gives food, the clever son takes it, then cries to get more." Another said, "It is better to have something than nothing."

Other Ethiopian translators said:

"People need Scripture now!"

"The Spirit of God is at work. God is in control. He is giving them His Word!"

"We do our best, and God does His best."

"Quality is being kept."

"Their translation quality is better than what I did myself."

"Foreigners always think they know better."

"The local Christians can do this work."

"Some projects take a long time, waste a lot of money, and produce nothing. MAST puts Scripture in the hands of the people today. That makes me rejoice!"

"MAST reflects the urgency of the gospel."

In describing MAST teamwork one said, "Fifty lemons is a heavy burden for one man, but for fifty men it is only an aroma." Another said, "If possible, everyone should participate!"

"It is important for even a single person to hear God's Word."

"It's timely."

"The people in the community must have the last word."

"Bible translation is the work of the church."

The Communities' Response

During the two-week workshop, four of the languages completed the book of Mark. The fifth language, Ch'ara, had recorded eleven chapters of Mark. The Inor team also completed Romans. The Gayil completed Galatians.

This is the first Scripture in history for these languages.

Several churches from these language groups gathered in Awassa for the closing session of the workshop. Hundreds of people gathered to lay hands on the Wycliffe Ethiopia team, praising God and commissioning them to continue the work of Bible translation in Ethiopia until every language has Scripture.

The international observers joined in the celebration. "Wycliffe Ethiopia has done a great job and worked wisely. We are proud of you!"

MAST is a MUST!

During the closing session the Deputy General Secretary of the Kale Heywet denomination, Dr. Woyita Woza Olla, took the platform and summed up the Ethiopian evaluation of MAST with a simple, but powerful, phrase, "MAST is a <u>must</u>!"

This phrase is being repeated in English, and translated into hundreds of new languages, as the rallying cry for church-centered Bible translation.

Tefera, Wycliffe Ethiopia's Executive Director, says, "What is happening in Ethiopia is a miracle! We are not going back. This movement is not going to be stopped. Wycliffe Ethiopia is here to serve the church. We will go forward and make MAST our own."

There are still more than seventy languages in Ethiopia without the Bible.

"MAST is a must!"

Chapter Seven

THE PHILIPPINES

H unters and gatherers lived off the rich flora and fauna of the tropical rainforests. Warrior tribes contested control of the plains. Mountains yielded their mineral wealth to generations of skilled craftsmen. Coastal cities grew on sheltered harbors. Long before European explorers arrived, the Philippine islands were well known to ocean-going traders from nearby places we now call Japan, Indonesia, China, Thailand, Vietnam, Taiwan, and India. The fabric of contemporary cultures in the Philippines includes threads and patterns from all of these people and places. Colonial Spanish, and more recently American, influences overlay these traditional foundations.

Animism, ancestor worship, and occult religious practices reflected the worldview of the local people for much of their history. Buddhism and Hinduism from surrounding regions began exerting influence during the sixth century. By the 1300s, both Christianity and Islam had reached the Philippines through Indian and Arab traders.

In 1521 Ferdinand Magellan arrived during his search for a westward passage to the Maluku Islands on behalf of Spain. Not long after his arrival, he was killed during a battle between local rivals. After his compatriots reached the Malukus and returned home, Spain and Portugal negotiated a treaty granting the Philippines to Spain and the Malukus to Portugal. Neither the Filipinos nor the Indonesians agreed to this treaty.

Forty-four years later, Spanish settlers from Mexico established their first settlement on Cebu Island in the central Philippines. Catholic missionaries built schools, hospitals, and churches as they ministered to the local people. However, the Filipinos resisted the Spanish *encomienda* system of paying economic tribute as well as religious conversion. Spanish control of the Philippines continued for more than three centuries, until 1898.

Early Bible Translation

Spanish Jewish immigrants privately funded translations of Scripture portions into Spanish as early as 1430. The complete Ferrera Bible was published in 1553. The popular Reina-Valera translation of the Bible in Spanish was published in 1602. Spanish friars translated Scripture portions into Tagalog, one of the major indigenous languages of the Philippines, in 1593.

However, throughout the era of Spanish control Filipinos were forbidden to own Bibles. Unauthorized translations by missionaries into local languages were destroyed when discovered.

American Intervention

During the late nineteenth century, national independence movements in the Philippines gained strength. These erupted into armed rebellion against the Spanish government in 1896. The next year the revolutionaries and the government agreed to a pact which reduced the overt hostilities but did not result in Philippine independence.

Meanwhile, on the other side of the globe, tensions were growing between the United States and Spain. Cuban revolutionary movements against Spain were gaining strength. The United States was pressuring Spain diplomatically to recognize Cuban independence. When the U.S.S. Maine exploded, and sank, under mysterious circumstances in Havana Harbor, the United States Navy responded with a naval blockade of the harbor and military support for the Cuban insurgents.

Within weeks, the U.S. Navy's Asiatic fleet increased the pressure on Spain by attacking, and defeating, the Spanish navy in the Battle of Manila Bay. The Filipino revolutionaries seized this opportunity to consolidate their control of nearly all of the Philippines, with the exception of Manila. Spain eventually ceded control of the Philippines to the United States in the Treaty of Paris. Not surprisingly, the Filipino leaders objected to the terms of this treaty, resulting in the Philippine-American War from 1899-1902 and continuing tensions for decades.

In the midst of this turmoil, several important things happened. First, the Americans implemented the separation of church and state. One key byproduct of this was that Filipinos could now legally own Bibles. A related byproduct of this was that Bible translations in Philippine majority languages moved forward. The first Protestant Bible in Tagalog, *Ang Biblia*, was published in 1905. The Ilocano Bible translation was completed in 1909. The Cebuano, *Bugna*, Bible was completed by Protestant missionaries in 1917.

Ten hours after the Japanese attack on Pearl Harbor on December 7, 1941, the Japanese invasion of the Philippines began. Without effective air cover, the U.S. Navy withdrew from the Philippines to distance themselves from the Japanese. Within a few months, the Japanese controlled much of the Philippines. Filipino guerilla resistance, supported intermittently by the United States, continued throughout three years of Japanese occupation. The U.S. Navy returned with strength in late 1944, overpowering the Japanese forces. The Treaty of Manila formalized the United States' recognition of the Philippines as a sovereign nation in 1946.

A New Season

Following World War II, the Protestant missionary movement surged. European and American soldiers, including many Christians, returned from war with a practical understanding of global cultural and language diversity. This was especially the case in relation to Pacific nations. By the mid-1950s Bible translation efforts were beginning in dozens of minority languages throughout the Pacific, including the Philippines.

As Filipino Protestant churches spread and matured their own vision for getting God's Word into minority languages increased. By the 1980s an indigenous Bible translation effort had begun. An influential pastor, Dr. Luis Pantoja, Sr. of Greenhills Christian Fellowship, saw that Filipino Christians could be strategic partners in the ministry of Bible translation throughout the world. Through his vision, Wycliffe Philippines was formed in 2007.

As a new partner in Bible translation, Wycliffe Philippines had no history shaping their vision. From their earliest days, the board of directors discussed the potential for technology and innovation to accelerate Bible translation. They imagined online virtual Bible translation and wiki collaboration via the Internet. In their words, "How can we continue with Bible translation requiring twenty to thirty years in this day and age of technology?" Their constant lookout for innovations in Bible translation led Simoun Ung, Board Chairman, to describe the maverick nature of Wycliffe Philippines as "a raging bull in the china shop of Bible translation."

The Priority of Orality

Dr. Romerlito (Romer) Macalinao was appointed as the first Executive Director of Wycliffe Philippines. His background included three decades in church pastoral leadership, a Masters degree in Christian Education, and a Doctoral degree in Adult and Continuing Education. During these years he also gained extensive experience with formal and nonformal education.

One of the first things that caught Dr. Romer's attention was that most of the remaining people groups without Scripture are oral learners. Facing this reality, he championed the need for an oral strategy for Bible translation. It took some time for him to persuade others that this was the right direction for Wycliffe Philippines, but as they took steps of faith they saw God's hand at work. Dr. Romer's background in education enabled him to lead the Wycliffe Philippines team to develop an orality-based training curriculum to equip Filipino cross-cultural missionaries to do language and culture-based church planting. They called their framework the Bible Translation Continuum—from spoken to written, oral to literate, and audio to print.

MAST Theory and Practice

In God's providence, Dr. Romer's Manila office was next to the office of Wycliffe Associates Asia Area Director, Mark Foster. Dr. Romer was very familiar with the physical and technical infrastructure, and volunteer support, Wycliffe Associates provided to Bible translation partners worldwide. Wycliffe Associates provided some computer resources for Wycliffe Philippines, and Wycliffe Philippines facilitated Wycliffe Associates' banking arrangements for personnel in Asia.

One day in 2014 Mark and Dr. Romer had lunch together. Bible translation was naturally the topic of discussion over lunch. Mark mentioned that Wycliffe Associates was testing a new approach to Bible translation called Mobilized Assistance Supporting Translation. Since Dr. Romer was always on the lookout for innovation, this caught his attention. When he then heard that MAST was designed by a professional language-learning specialist his curiosity increased even more. Dr. Romer said, "Get me the documentation. I need to learn more about this." So, Mark put him in contact with Dan.

As Dr. Romer read of the educational theories, brain research, and language learning principles behind MAST they resonated deeply with him. These were the same principles he had learned and honed during his years in Christian education. He also knew from experience that the distance between theory and practice could be significant. So he told Mark, "I need to see MAST work firsthand."

Plans came together for Wycliffe Philippines' first MAST workshop in August 2015. Because of their interest in orality, the decision was made to begin by using MAST to translate the fifty Open Bible Stories for six languages in Mindanao. When Dr. Romer learned more about the strategy to create open-license Bible translation resources in majority gateway languages he added the Tagalog, Ilocano, and Cebuano languages to the event. Experienced Bible translators and translation consultants participated and evaluated the MAST results by the local translators in each language. Their conclusion was simple—MAST worked. It fit their vision and values. The excitement and engagement of Christians from these communities were obvious. Tears ran down their cheeks as they experienced Bible translation firsthand.

Moving Forward

The importance of having open-license Bible translation resources in gateway languages for the Philippines was clear. Wycliffe Philippines immediately began recruiting translators to use MAST to translate the Unlocked English Bible into Tagalog, Ilocano, and Cebuano. The enthusiasm of the Filipino church in creating these tools was encouraging.

Even as the local passion grew, criticism began surfacing from some of Wycliffe Philippines' other partners in Bible translation. MAST was new and unorthodox. They exhorted Dr. Romer to stick with conventional translation strategies. He responded by championing MAST and inviting the skeptics to join the movement. Wycliffe Philippines embraced MAST and pressed forward with the Philippines gateway translations.

In September 2016 Dr. Romer was traveling east for meetings of the International Orality Network. At the same time, Dan was traveling west to lead MAST workshops in Asia. Their paths crossed in Seattle, so they agreed to meet to discuss follow-up from the recent MAST workshop in the Philippines. Dr. Romer shared his heart for the Bibleless people groups and unreached nations of Southeast Asia. Dan's heart resonated with Dr. Romer's vision. They spent the day dreaming of how the entire region of Southeast Asia might break out of Bible poverty. A plan emerged in which Wycliffe Philippines would have a regional role in advancing Bible translation beyond their own borders. The vision of Filipinos serving the nations in Bible translation was coming to fruition.

In the closing months of 2016, Dan traveled to the Philippines to lead Advanced Theory Training on MAST for the Wycliffe Philippines team. This training explained the educational and language-learning principles that form the theoretical foundation of MAST. Because of Dr. Romer's contacts throughout Southeast Asia, Wycliffe Philippines team members began facilitating MAST workshops in Myanmar, Thailand, and other Southeast Asian countries.

More Languages

Recent research counted the total languages in the Philippines at 187, with just twenty-three languages that still needed Bible translation. It turns out that Filipinos count the needs differently.

Through their work on gateway languages, the Wycliffe Philippines team built a solid foundation of experience in facilitating MAST workshops. Because of their local church relationships, they invited more Bibleless language groups to begin translating Scripture. During the past two years, Wycliffe Philippines hosted a dozen MAST workshops and enabled thirteen Filipino languages to begin Bible translation for their people. Most of these are New Testament translations, but Old Testament translations are also moving forward. From their perspective, there are still dozens of Filipino languages to serve with MAST, as well as hundreds of languages throughout Southeast Asia—where Filipinos are partners in making disciples of the nations through Bible translation. Wycliffe Philippines uses Bible Translation Recording Kits to facilitate oral translations from audio sources, has begun testing Virtual MAST online collaboration tools to link translation teams that are separated by long distances. They are anxious to apply every tool and strategy to advance Bible translation within their circles.

Dr. Romer's Exhortation

In February 2017 I had the opportunity to meet Dr. Romer for the first time. We met at a gathering of leaders in Bible translation from the global South and East. There were a couple dozen leaders from across Africa, Asia, and the Pacific. Dr. Romer and his Translation Manager, Tano Emboc, represented the Philippines at these meetings. Dan and I were invited to listen, answer questions about MAST, and encourage our brothers and sisters in their leadership of Bible translation.

By that time all of these international partners knew about MAST, and most had put it to work successfully in their countries. Many of these partners also had much longer history and experience in Bible translation than Wycliffe Philippines. Some had been involved in Bible translation for more than forty years. All are experts in languages and cultures in their own countries.

Each leader gave a report on the progress of Bible translation in his country and commented on his experiences with MAST. One of the challenges they all faced was how to adapt their prior strategies and structures to the new translation method. Some kept their prior structures and simply added MAST to their existing strategies. Others made significant changes to their structures to support MAST. Each leader described the reasons and benefits for their choices. Dr. Romer was among the last to report. He stood to address his partners and colleagues and said, "We shouldn't put new wine into old wineskins." He challenged everyone to reconsider their choices in order to maximize the blessing of MAST to those still without God's Word.

Alma May Llorca

"I am so grateful to God because I had a glimpse of what may happen to the translators after the workshop. In the early stage of the project I was only thinking of myself, that serving as a translator will help me to understand deeper the truth concerning God and my relationship with Him will be strengthened. But after the workshop I've had a change of mind and heart. It's not all about me, but all for the glory and expansion of the kingdom of God. Everyone should know and hear the Word of God."

Molly Balindong

"I was assigned to the tribe of Mandaya. Their villages had just been hit by a storm, their houses were flooded, and they had lost their possessions. When I found out about this I expected that these people would be distressed and unmotivated when I met them and that it could be a problem for the entire workshop. On the first day, I had the chance to get to know them and introduce myself. Opposite to what I expected, they were so excited about the workshop! One lady gave her testimony, telling us that she is seventy years old. She didn't expect to be able to join the workshop because she's old and felt like she's not useful anymore, but she was so glad about being able to be there despite her age. There were two pastors on the team. They had such powerful and encouraging words for the translation team. One high school student took a long abscncc from school to join in. It was a blessing because I was expecting to be the one to lift their souls, but instead they were the ones who lifted mine. Seeing them so excited about translating the Word of God—despite the troubles that they had back home—surprised me. These people have blessed me. They had all the reasons to be distressed and complain about life, and say 'no' to the call of God, but instead they were thankful, passionate, and they willingly came to the workshop."

Charity Guinita

"God really pushed me to come out of my comfort zone and let me experience new things—which I do not usually do. He helped me conquer my greatest fear of being ashamed to face many people. He used me and put me on the right track. My prayer was to be more useful in His ministry so I could teach others and help them know more about God. Sometimes I feel like I am useless because, unlike others, I have not led churches or large groups. But I know He has prepared something for me. Helping in the workshop required patience and humility. Because I do not easily mingle with others, some people see me as *maldita* [strict]. But God's grace is abundant. Seeing them respond and doing translation really broke my heart. They helped their community to know more about God by using their heart language. They said that translation is so difficult, but also fulfilling. After the workshop I felt drained and weak, but thinking how God had worked really gave me courage and strength to continue to do what God wants me to do. God's great commission is to proclaim his word to everyone, everywhere."

Darryl Lasquite

"The happenings in workshops that I have attended were overwhelming. While I was facilitating the Talacognon tribe, I heard their unique stories about themselves that inspired me a lot and challenged me to continue serving the Lord. I heard the testimony of one young man, Jeymark, who was twenty years old. His foot was twisted after being run over by a truck, and his tongue was distorted so he can't speak clearly. He has many problems with his body but he strives so hard to help his team and be able to translate many passages of Scriptures into his mother tongue so that his tribe will be helped. His life is challenging but it never stopped him from continuing to work for the Lord. I felt so blessed seeing him dancing even though his foot is twisted. He also sings and plays instruments despite his voice impairment. He said to me that he was so grateful to the Lord because it has been a long time that his people were longing for Scripture in their heart language—and this is the fulfillment of their dreams! I invested time with them and taught them many things about MAST in order to empower them to do the translation by themselves. I am strengthened, growing in faith, and inspired because of them. My prayer is that all languages will translate Scripture into their heart language and that many people will come to Christ before He returns. This will fulfill the promise that when the gospel is preached to every language and nation, Christ will return."

Helen Thundas

"It was He who gave some to be apostles, some to be prophets, some to be evangelists, and some to be pastors and teachers, to prepare God's people for works of service, so that the body of Christ may be built up until we all reach unity in the faith and in the knowledge of the Son of God and become mature, attaining the whole measure of the fullness of Christ." Ephesians 4:11-13 NIV

"I was so blessed to be one of the facilitators for the Agusan workshop. I thank God for the opportunity He gave me, not only to share knowledge about MAST but also to learn many things throughout the workshop. When I received the text message inviting me to be one of the facilitators I was so happy. But I asked God, Why me? I felt unqualified to do the task but when I was there I was so glad to meet the Pangyan, Bunawanon, and Talacognon tribal groups. I saw the excitement of those participants and saw their willingness to translate the Bible in their own language.

I appreciate the compassion and joy of those translators to work to have the Bible in their own dialect even though they were not paid any money. I was blessed by the testimony of Mr. Mark, a Talcognon translator who is physically inca- pacitated, but he is willing to offer his life to the work of God. He said sometimes he questioned God about his situ- ation, and of all the people in the world—why him? But he realized the love of God through his situation. That's why he fully offered his time to the ministry of God. Ate Grace, a Bunawanon translator said, 'If you want to prioritize the will of God, you can not forsake adversity. I have unspeak- able joy that I participated in Bible translation.' These are the people who motivate and challenge me to pursue what I have started with MAST."

Monie Chiong

Monie Chiong is the Field Operations Director of Wycliffe Philippines and a senior consultant on Scripture engage- ment. Together with his wife, Marianne, he was a Bible translator for the Agta and Paranan people. As previous members of The Navigators, their commitment to discipling leaders was woven into their work as Bible translators. He discipled his language assistants, who eventually became pastors. He catalyzed a church planting movement among the Agta and Paranan. This led him to form Christian Missions to the Unreached and the Indigenous Christian Churches of the Philippines.

He recounts his first exposure to MAST during the MAST Open Bible Stories workshop held at the Language and Culture Institute in Manila in August 2015. "During that workshop, my impression was that it was a simplified translation methodology. I was amazed that the computer program could record the translated stories orally. From my background as a trained translator, I saw the eight steps of MAST as very similar to what I had done—but simpli- fied. The local people did it with a short amount of training. I had worked with a nomadic people group and it took me a long time to train the people to translate. I thought they must be literate first. So, we sent them to school before we trained them to translate. After a long time, they assumed the translation work." Like many others with experience in Bible translation, Monie discovered that MAST included the mother-tongue speakers from the very beginning and produced accurate results.

Monie and the rest of the MAST team of Wycliffe Philippines use the Tagalog, Ilocano, and Cebuano gateway translations as source texts for MAST workshops among minority people groups. He said, "My later involvement in minority translations made me excited that local people can now have their Bible. The local churches and communities are empowered to translate and approve it, either in oral or written form. Since the translation belongs to the people, and it is free, this makes Scripture engagement a reality in any Bible Translation initiative."

Tano Emboc

Tano Emboc is the Translation Manager for Wycliffe Philippines. He grew up in the mountains of Bukidnon, in the Southern Philippines, speaking Matigsalug. His mother was a Christian. His father was an animist who persecuted his wife because of her faith. Because the Bible was not yet translated into Matigsalug, Tano's first Bible was in the local majority language, Cebuano. Although Cebuano was not his heart language, he taught himself to read it by mimicking his cousin, a pastor. Within two months he could read Cebuano without any assistance. As he read he was drawn closer to God. He carried the Bible with him everywhere he went, reading whenever he had a spare moment. He calls the Bible, "My first teacher."

Throughout Tano's childhood and adolescence, he sensed the battle for his soul between animism and the Spirit of God. Although he put his faith in Christ, he sometimes compromised his faith to escape beatings from his father or ridicule from his peers. The village leaders considered Christianity a Western religion, threatening to their culture. God totally changed his life when he joined a Bible translation team at the age of twenty-one.

"God changed everything in me and strengthened me to stand firm for Him. I served as a translator for eleven years and God remained faithful to me and to all that He entrusted to me. Bible translation is a unique form of God's ministry because it penetrates to the root of the culture through the heart language. When the Biblical meaning is understood very well by the translators and assimilated appropriately into the other language the impact is overwhelming. It touches the very inner parts of the person like God is intimately communicating Himself with that person in the language his lips love to use. When I first touched my Bible in Matigsalug my heart was stirred and I nearly cried because of joy which cannot be defined."

Tano has led more than ten MAST workshops and is responsible for training local translators to use MAST. "We have diverse people helping in translation work. All of them are believers at different stages, but we are all growing every day. Those mature older Christians are guiding the new believers. Most of the translators are pastors. We always start our workshops listening to the Word of God, giving encouragement to each other, and praising the Lord for everything He has done for us."

After using other translation strategies for many years, Tano described the blessing of MAST for local languages. "MAST is a must approach. It is simple, yet effective. It helps make translation easy for the translators. I like it a lot. Its impact on the people being served is overwhelming. When the church is engaged, empowered to do Bible translation, the impact is beyond description because the Spirit of God puts the Word in the person's heart and ministers to him in the language that person understands most. MAST allows people to be part of the process in the early stages and continually empowered to own, use, sustain, and take accountability for the work. This is the unique element of MAST that I see in my context. I see people changing and empowered to be part of the work in building the kingdom of God.

It is my prayer to the Lord that the tribal people like me will see the light of God's salvation through MAST, and the Lord will continue to use me in serving the people through Bible translation. I want the world to know that the Word of the Lord gives hope to the hopeless, brings joy and comfort to the desperate, and provides freedom and life to those who are living in the dark world. I would encourage every believer around the world to come, support, and bring the free gift of salvation to the less-privileged, unfortunate, and persecuted people of the world—and let them see the light of God's salvation. God loves these people, and they need His Word."

Chapter Eight

DARK ISLAND

I t is one of the largest unevangelized islands on earth. It has been wracked by political and religious unrest for more than three centuries. For much of this time access by foreigners, particularly Christian missionaries, has been extremely limited. With a population over 50 million, and with more than 50 unique languages spoken, it has been a high priority for Bible translation for many years. Yet progress has been very limited, and sometimes temporary. At one point all known copies of the New Testament in one minority language were seized by local authorities and burned. Islamic Sharia law has periodically been invoked as a way to intimidate, persecute, and control the local Christians.

Turning Back the Pages of Time

Imagine the world two hundred years ago. The twenty states of the USA extended only as far west as the Mississippi River. European colonialism had reached past the Americas to Asia but had not yet overpowered Africa. Most oceanic transportation was still on wooden sailing ships, but iron steamships were visible on the horizon. During the previous thousand years, Islam had spread from the Middle East to both the Atlantic and Pacific.

While the indigenous tribes were traditional animists, on Dark Island Islam had already been growing for five hundred years. Much of the land had been politically divided into Islamic Sultanates. Many of the islanders accepted the political authority and the trade benefits that came with it. But as with many people, the imposition of strict laws stirred rebellion against the political powers.

Into this complex local power struggle an unlikely ally surfaced for one small people group.

Colonial Power

Several centuries after the Muslims, European trading companies arrived in this region in search of natural resources. By the late sixteenth century the challenges of managing global commerce exceeded the management capabilities of many of these companies. So, the home nations of these companies took over their assets and attempted to establish colonial authority. Their efforts had mixed results.

While the colonial power effectively controlled nearby islands, control of the Dark Island was frequently contested. In the early 1800s local enforcement of Sharia law led the Coffee people to turn to the colonial army for protection and relief. The Europeans seized this opportunity to establish a strategic military post in the center of the contested region. The subsequent battles for control occupied the next century and only resulted in temporary control by the various contenders.

Good News

Christian chaplains accompanied the European army troops as they established their outposts. In addition to ministering to the needs of the troops, the chaplains naturally began ministering to the needs of the Coffee people. Because the army had been invited into this region, the Coffee people never viewed their presence as a foreign occupation. The Europeans were their defenders. Perhaps because of this alliance, the Coffee people were open and interested to learn from the Europeans.

When the Christian chaplains told the Coffee people that God had sent His Son, Jesus, to break the power of evil over their lives—they knew this was good news. Traditional religion was their own attempt to manipulate the occult powers that surrounded them. But generations of experience had proven their inability to escape the grip of evil. Coffee families began turning to Christ.

In the subsequent years, Mennonite missionary families from Europe arrived in the Coffee community. They established schools and medical clinics to serve the local people. Unlike the colonial army chaplains and troops that moved from post to post, these missionaries settled permanently. They invested their lives as a testimony of God's love for the Coffee people.

In 1834 the first Christian church was built in the Coffee community. For more than a century only European Bible translations were available to this church. Colonial governance came to an end there at the close of World War II. In the late twentieth century, a Bible translation was completed in the official national language but it wasn't until 2016 that the Coffee people began to translate the Bible into their own heart language. Getting to that point took a lot of prayer and perseverance.

Looking for An Opportunity to Serve

Jan and I had visited this country during the mid-1990s, but we were unable to visit Dark Island. We spent time in the capital city and visited three other major islands to connect with Christian missionary work there, but Dark Island was closed.

When I came to Wycliffe Associates in 2000 I discovered that this nation was a very high priority for Bible translation with several hundred languages still without a single verse of Scripture. I learned that we had a staff family assigned to a partner organization on one of the major islands, managing construction projects related to a major center for foreigners working in Bible translation. We made several attempts to increase volunteer support for Bible translation in the country but the political limitations on work permits limited our opportunities to serve.

Violence Strikes

Twenty years earlier, on another island of this country, Wycliffe Associates built a Bible translation center that included more than a dozen buildings. I learned this when that center was overrun by Muslim extremists intent on killing all of the Christians on their island. As this violence erupted the foreign missionaries working in Bible translation evacuated with only the clothes on their backs. All of their personal possessions and professional equipment was left behind.

The implications for Bible translation in this country were devastating. As I conferred with our international partners I soon learned that there was no contingency plan in place to assist these families or reestablish the Bible translations that were interrupted. Wycliffe Associates stepped in to help. We established a Missionary 911 Emergency Fund and invited our constituents to respond financially. Because of the generous response, every missionary family was safely relocated and resupplied to enable them to resume their translation work almost immediately. Many of these families moved to a neighboring country where Wycliffe Associates then built offices, a school, and expanded housing.

During the following years, it was estimated that 9,000 people were killed and hundreds of thousands of local people were displaced from their homes and businesses in this region. On the surface this was a huge setback to Bible translation, but it also increased Wycliffe Associates' direct engagement and positioned us to respond when circumstances changed on Dark Island.

Severe Disaster Strikes

At the end of 2004 the third-largest earthquake in recorded history, with the longest duration ever recorded, devastated Dark Island. Geologists estimate the force as equivalent to more than 23,000 atomic bombs. The resulting tsunami killed 170,000 people and left more than 500,000 homeless on Dark Island.

This was the greatest disaster in recorded history for this region. Because there was no work in process on Dark Island there was no immediate impact on Bible translation. But the disaster created the opportunity to respond compassionately to the local people and begin building relationships and experience for future translation work. In the following years, we worked with local organizations to rebuild homes that were destroyed by the tsunami. Initially, these collaborations seemed promising to create natural transitions from physical ministry to spiritual ministry. However, the political limitations on long-term assignment of Bible translators continued to frustrate our efforts to reach local language communities.

Watching, Praying, and God Answers

As we continued praying and searching for opportunities to advance Bible translation in this nation a decade passed. It was deeply disappointing for me, but in hindsight it seems that the timing wasn't right.

Then God intervened in two unexpected ways.

First, a small group of Christians in a country thousands of miles away had the faith and boldness to begin translating the Bible in a new way—under the authority of local church leaders. This new translation strategy, called MAST, did not depend on the long-term presence of foreign missionaries. Instead, it engaged the people and knowledge God had already positioned within the local church. This meant that the limitation on long-term missionaries was no longer an obstacle to Bible translation on Dark Island.

Second, God connected us with someone He had strategically positioned on Dark Island decades earlier—the son of a Bible translator, married to a local Christian.

A Plan Develops

Brent Ropp, Wycliffe Associates' Vice-President of Operations, flew to Dark Island in early 2014 to meet with Sam[6] and explore ways to begin Bible translation from a local perspective. Merging Sam into our Operations team required some months of preparation and transition, but during these months a plan began to coalesce with multiple partner organizations that would launch Bible translations in a cluster of nine related languages on Dark Island—bringing God's Word to over 2.8 million people.

In order to begin building relationships in one key location, Sam and his wife rented a plot of farmland and planted potatoes. During the weeks of cultivating the emerging shoots, they met several local farmers. Selling the crop in the local market gave them further opportunities to make friends and consider the best way to launch Bible translation for these people.

Initial enthusiasm for this plan ran high. It looked like the breakthrough we had been praying for. But as soon as the plan came together, it began falling apart. Part of the challenge was in trying to balance and integrate the priorities of multiple partner organizations. While the end goal of getting Scripture to the people was unanimous, the means of pursuing that goal were not. Based on the growth

---

[6] A pseudonym.

and success of the MAST strategy during 2014, Wycliffe Associates advocated the recruitment of local Christian translators working under local church authority. As an initial project, the other partners preferred to maintain external management of the translations. In addition, division developed within our own team as various strategies and priorities were weighed in an attempt to reconcile multiple viewpoints. Satan was sowing discord.

Just before the launch of these nine translations, in early 2015, it became clear that this plan was not going to happen.

More Prayer

Brent had already planned to return to Dark Island to connect with Sam for the launch of the cluster project. Instead of excitement for the beginning of a new project, Brent landed with a heavy heart and no clear path forward. As he met with Sam and a few others Brent described the translation breakthroughs that God was enabling through MAST in Asia, Africa, and the Middle East. It seemed as though God was moving everywhere but on Dark Island.

But Brent refused to believe it. Instead, he rallied the small group to prayer, asking God to make a way where there seemed to be no way.

A Long Night

That night Brent returned to the humble rural guest house and fell asleep, exhausted. But while Brent slept, Sam and his friends could not. Instead, they spent the night thinking about the few believers they knew on Dark Island. Each time they thought of a name they made a cell call to see if they could reach their contacts. They then explained that they were looking for people interested in translating God's Word into the languages of Dark Island. One contact became two. Two contacts became four. As phones continued to ring, and be answered throughout the night, God began to light the path forward.

Answered Prayers

When Brent awoke the next morning he was shocked to hear of the connections Sam had made overnight. With a glimmer of encouragement, Brent boarded a flight to a nearby island for another exploratory meeting.

Within a few hours after landing, Brent found himself in a conversation with the former President of a local Christian seminary. As Brent described the vision and challenges of getting Scripture into the languages of Dark Island, this leader shared that he knew a student that was planting churches on Dark Island. A second conversation with a local Christian leader turned up another contact there. Calls and email began crossing the water to confirm these connections. Within just a few days local church partners were identified in nine strategic locations on Dark Island.

God had already prepared the path for Bible translation, as only He could, by positioning local Christians in places foreigners could not go.

People of the Interior

During the spring and summer of 2015, Sam and his local team traveled extensively throughout Dark Island to follow up in person with the Christian contacts that had surfaced. In each case the initial contacts introduced additional friends, expanding the network of people interested in seeing Bible translation begin. Evangelists confirmed the lack of Scripture, the locations of indigenous churches, and the spiritual needs of the local people.

In the south central region of Dark Island, a nomadic tribe of 15,000 people hunt and gather food for survival. Their love of pork proved to be a practical barrier to the entry of Islam, so most of them continued to follow traditional animistic beliefs and practices. Because of their primitive existence they have been pursued and exploited by outsiders, leaving them extremely wary of foreigners. But the good news of the gospel came through national evangelists and churches are being planted. With several hundred believers, they are technically considered a reached people group. But they have no Scripture in their language.

When they learned that we wanted to help them translate God's Word into their language they were very interested. They offered their cement block church building as the best place for a MAST workshop. A very basic dormitory nearby could host visitors. Several men in the church volunteered to be translators but hunting would have to be included in the workshop schedule in order to support their families. Since few read or write, the translation would need to be from an audio source to an oral recording. They wanted to begin with the book of Mark.

The Coastal People

Further north a group of more than 200,000 live in the coastal swamps and smaller islands. The region is so remote and inhospitable that few outsiders are even aware that people inhabit the area. They live on sago, a starch similar to tapioca, and wild pig. Again, their reliance on pork as a staple led them to reject Islam. National Christian evangelists have ministered among the Coastal people for two decades, resulting in a thriving church of several thousand. They have been praying, and waiting, for more than ten years to have God's Word in their language. When they learned that we were willing to help them translate the Bible they immediately saw this as God's answer to their prayers.

A single dirt road leads from the nearest city into the coastal region. Bicycles navigate the driest paths while sandaled feet walk the shallows. From the end of the road, the only access to their islands is by boat.

Pastor O has lived ten years with the Coastal people. Not long after he arrived in the region he was struck by lightning while sitting on the front porch of his home. His house caught fire and he nearly lost his life. The local people heard the thunder, saw the ball of fire, and rescued him from the flames. His body was charred black. Blood was oozing from his eyes, ears, and nose. He was unconscious and not breathing. Some of the Christian believers laid hands on him and prayed for God to spare his life. When they opened their eyes Pastor O began breathing! They took him by boat to a hospital for medical care for his burns. In just one week he was released and returned to the village. The Coastal people were convinced that someone had tried to kill Pastor O with black magic. But the obvious power of God to protect and heal Pastor O convinced hundreds to give their lives to Christ!

The first planning meeting for Bible translation in this language included eleven men and women from three different Coastal villages. Some had traveled two days to attend the meeting. As they discussed the details surrounding a MAST workshop the local believers were overcome with joy at the prospect of having God's Word in their language. One young man said, "We are nobody in the eyes of this country and our government. We do not count, and we have nothing. No one knows we even exist! But, if we have God's Word in our language, we will finally feel like we have something special and belong to the world community!"

Far North

As the survey of language communities turned further north the challenges increased. While there are several large language groups without Scripture, the evangelists living and working in this region are all from neighboring tribes. They speak the local languages fluently but are still outsiders. The evangelists are ready, willing, and able to begin translation in these languages. Progress will be difficult due to the fact that no churches exist in this region. Literacy is extremely low, so oral translations will be essential for reaching the people.

Finding the Coffee People

From the beginning of our efforts to begin Bible translation on Dark Island, we were aware of the Coffee people. With more than a million speakers, several thousand Christian believers, and no Scripture, it seemed that God had prepared them to begin Bible translation on Dark Island. Interestingly, the Coffee people are closely connected to the people we served following the earthquake in 2004. A believer from this group attended the very first meeting to discuss launching new translations in April of 2015. After a couple site visits during late 2015, the local church selected fifteen Christians to begin translation. A MAST workshop was set for early 2016.

The Journey

After a dozen years of praying, planning, and waiting I was excited to see MAST launch Bible translation on Dark Island. This would be only my second opportunity to see MAST bring Scripture to people who had waited too long to hear God speak their language.

As I flew toward the gathering I carried with me all the misperceptions that had accumulated in my heart and mind during years of frustration. I knew the reputation of the majority Muslim population in the region. Based on previous travels to Islamic countries I expected severe security limitations. Mentally, emotionally, and spiritually I prepared for hostile threats to our efforts.

My first clue that my perceptions were instead misperceptions came when my flight landed at the capital city and I made the connection for my final leg to Dark Island. I expected to be the only foreigner on the flight. Instead, I was surprised to see a dozen foreigners converging at the departure desk—checking their surfboards as baggage! I was also surprised the local men and women checking in for the flight were not in robes and turbans. They wore western clothing. I was confused.

Upon arrival in the provincial capital, I caught a cab to the hotel. Roads and traffic often provide the first impression of a new place. In this case, I was very impressed. The roads and vehicles were well maintained and traffic flowed smoothly. In most of the places I travel this is not the case, so the differences stood out positively. I arrived late morning local time, so the challenge for the first day was to recover from the travel and adapt to the local time zone. Brent's flight arrived later in the day, so I had some time to adjust.

After sitting in cramped seats and eating airline food I often look for someplace to exercise. At this hotel the exercise room happened to be on the roof, so I ventured up several flights of stairs to check it out. As I emerged on the rooftop the skyline of the surrounding city drew my eyes. That's when another shock hit me. As I surveyed the rooftops the most striking view was of Christian crosses pointing toward the sky. There were at least a dozen crosses visible. To be sure, there were also dozens of Islamic crescent moons atop neighborhood mosques. It was the public visibility of the Christian churches that shocked me. These were not hidden house churches. They were public meeting places.

My curiosity aroused, I descended the stairs and opted for a run through the city as my exercise. Twisting streets conspired to get me lost as I breathed in the sights and sounds of a new city. Pedestrians, traffic, mosques, parks, schools, and yes—churches defined the neighborhood. After several minutes the street turned abruptly to parallel the waterfront. I could see surfers to the south as I turned north. The hotels and restaurants looked just like their counterparts in Florida. The sea breeze tasted just like the Gulf breezes.

As I jogged through a congested commercial area I turned down a tree-lined side street and found myself in the midst of a crowd of pedestrians overflowing into the street from a large building—a church. Several hundred Christians were arriving and departing from church meetings on foot, on bicycles, motorcycles, and in cars. They were not hiding. They were not being monitored by police. They were not confronted by radical Muslims. They were coming and going as if they did it every day. I was shocked but elated!

When Brent arrived later we coordinated dinner and planned our departure for the next morning, then retired for the night. In the morning we met our driver and began the day-long drive north. After paralleling the coastline for several hours we turned toward the interior of the island. Coastal plains quickly gave way to foothills, and then mountains. The twisting road passed dozens of gorgeous vistas, peaks, valleys, lakes, and farms. The views were inspiring and time passed quickly.

Before I knew it we turned off the paved road onto a narrower dirt road. As the village at the intersection receded we wound between sparkling emerald fields of rice tended by elders permanently bent over at the waist. Coffee plantations dotted the surrounding hills. As our van rolled to a stop another shock hit me.

We stopped in front of a church building. I had wrongly assumed that the Coffee Christians would be less overt. Instead, I walked up to the church door and saw a plaque on the wall indicating that this church was founded—in 1834.

No matter how far I travel on the frontiers of Christianity, I always find that God has been there long before me.

MAST Underway

The Coffee translation team had been hard at work for a week by the time we arrived. Lori, the MAST facilitator, had preceded us and provided them the training they needed to start translation. The translators were divided into teams, each focusing on different books during the initial translation phase, then working through the quality checking steps in progressively larger groups. People from the nearby farms and village stopped by to share coffee with the translators and hear progress reports on the work. During the first week several New Testament books had already moved through the quality checking process, so enthusiasm was high as they worked to translate additional books.

One specific blessing of this location was reliable electricity. At the church the electricity powered three essentials; the coffee maker, the lights, and a printer. The translators did their initial work on paper with pens or pencils. These manuscripts were then input into a few laptop computers we had provided to support the team. Once the digital files were saved they printed proof copies to check the spelling, punctuation, and formatting. The limitations of this particular printer contributed to our later decision to include higher quality printers as resources for every MAST workshop.

I describe myself as a social coffee drinker. I've never really acquired the taste for it. But in cross-cultural situations, I gladly drink coffee with the local people. Brent, on the other hand, has never met a cup of coffee he didn't like. Not long after we arrived someone handed me a cup of the local brew—and I was, again, shocked! It tasted better than any coffee I've ever had!

Local Conversations

Since I didn't know the Coffee language I was not much help to the translation teams, so my conversations depended on a few of the nationals who were bilingual in English. One of these was the young pastor. She had a very young child and worked a second job in the village in addition to pastoring the church. I was interested to hear her perspective on MAST and the Bible translation process. She was very encouraged by the progress and quality of the translation she had assisted in checking. But she said something that had not previously occurred to me. She said that never before in the history of their church had so many of the Christians spent such a prolonged time studying, thinking, and praying about God's Word. As she considered the implications for the Christian community, her sense was that there would be a significant, immediate impact on the entire community because of the deep impact on the translators themselves. The long-term blessing of having Scripture in their own language would extend this impact to ever expanding circles in the community over the coming months and years. In her view, Bible translation had just ignited a spiritual renewal for her people!

One of the church elders offered to take us on a walking tour of the area around the church. Since most of the village was down the road, the tour didn't take long. The primary stop was the church cemetery. The elder described the history of the colonial army encamped in their village. My heart pounded as I realized that this army was from the country of my own forebears. I was fearful that people who looked like me had left a trail of violence and destruction. Despite this, I found the strength to admit my heritage. I waited nervously for his response. The silence felt heavy but was broken when the elder said, "No. Your people defended ours. We are indebted to them." My smile trembled through tears. He went on to explain how the army chaplains had told them about Jesus, and how European Mennonite missionaries came later to minister to the people and build the church. It was Brent's turn to tear up as he realized that his forebears had also had an impact for eternity here. The elder pointed to three graves unusually close together. They were the graves of a missionary mother and her twin babies. All three died during childbirth. I winced involuntarily, thinking of my daughters and grandsons—two of whom are twins.

Brent and I both wondered how two guys from the Midwest ended up walking in the footsteps of our forebears halfway around the world from our homes.

A Moral Dilemma

While we were with the Coffee people our local program manager, Sam, joined Brent and me to talk about questions surrounding our plans for additional MAST workshops throughout the island. He had done a lot of work to survey the needs and connect with Christians interested in translating Scripture. But he had deep concerns about our policy of asking local Christians to volunteer their time as translators. As a long-term local resident in the country, and on Dark Island, he was acutely aware of the economic hardships of the local people and felt that we had a moral obligation to pay the translators for their time. It was a policy choice that we had thought through carefully, and had tested in a broad range of locations and circumstances.

Without disagreeing about the poverty and need of the local people, we had learned through experience that when foreigners pay for work to be done the local people naturally see it as working for foreigners. The unfortunate result was that the local churches often saw Bible translation as owned by foreigners, and not their own. Also, in most cases Bible translations were copyrighted, and owned, by people outside the language community. Too often this left them without access to Scripture. We were intent on overcoming these historical limitations.

As I reasoned with Sam it became clear that this was a deep-seated principle on which we were not going to agree.

When that became clear to him he told me plainly that I was a heartless, unjust, and immoral person without respect or understanding of minority people. I was too narrowly focused on Bible translation and not compassionate for the poverty of the local people. So, he resigned on the spot.

That was one of the worst conversations of my life. He was very passionate, and it led me to several dark hours searching the corners of my heart. Naturally, I counseled with Brent as well. We talked about our policy, reflected on its development, and prayed for God's wisdom. Neither of us wanted to perpetuate a policy that would be harmful to local believers. We sought counsel from the national believers that were assisting to facilitate the MAST workshop. In the end, we concluded again that it is best for the local church to own their Bible translation. We continue to ask local Christians to volunteer their time as Bible translators and serve under the authority of the local church.

The Results

On Friday, January 29, 2016, around sixty Coffee believers gathered at their church to celebrate and dedicate eighteen books of their New Testament. Singing, testimonies, prayer, food, and coffee combined to express their thanksgiving for having God's Word in their heart language. As they closed their first MAST workshop they planned to break some weeks for harvest, then complete their New Testament in April 2016. Their vision is to immediately translate the Old Testament as well.

Their people had waited 182 years to begin something that took just two weeks to accomplish. 182 years. Almost two centuries. People had told them they could not do it. They were told they were unqualified. They were told they were unable, not intelligent enough, to do it. They were told they were not permitted to translate the Bible into their language. For 182 years they believed all of this, so they made do with Bibles in foreign languages.

As I departed Dark Island the next day I received an email from someone who had heard what was happening and went to great lengths to tell me that what the Coffee people had done was a mistake. This person had never met the Coffee people, and had never seen MAST in process, but condemned their translation.

But… the Coffee people did it. They now have God's Word in their language. God enabled them to do it. All we did was have the faith to tell them that He would.

Chapter Nine

BRAZIL

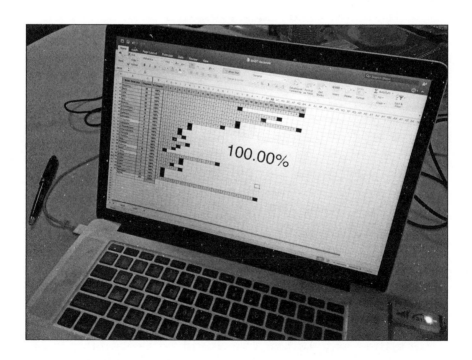

L ittle is known of the pre-colonial history of the region that is now Brazil. It is a vast and diverse tropical expanse, rich in resources, but a harsh environment for human survival. When Portuguese explorers landed in the region in the early 1500s, they encountered thousands of migrant tribes of hunters and gatherers. Tribal competition for survival often led to recurring warfare. Animism and occult religious practices, including cannibalism, were widespread.

During the early 1500s, Portugal was trading profitably with India and China and was slow in developing official trade with Brazil. This vacuum resulted in a chaotic conver-gence of international traders and opportunists plundering Brazil for some years. Many of the colonists were criminals expelled from Portugal.

By 1549, Jesuit missionaries migrated to coastal Brazil under a Papal mandate to evangelize the local population and educate the colonists. One of the pivotal early successes of the Jesuits occurred when they appealed for and received a royal decree prohibiting enslavement of the local people in 1570. Traders worked around this limitation by importing nearly five million African slaves into Brazil—more there than any other country in the world—further increasing the cultural diversity.

Within thirty years 100,000 Brazilians were affiliated with the Jesuits. Other Roman Catholic religious societies followed and expanded their influence for the next two centuries. By 1759 their religious influence was so perva-sive that the Portuguese governor forcibly expelled them in order to assert secular government authority in Brazil. In 1822 the Brazilian independence movement overthrew Portuguese colonial control. In 1889 their first constitution established freedom of religion and separation of church and state.

Bibles for Brazil

The earliest translation of Bible portions into Portuguese may have occurred at the request of King Dinis in Portugal during the early 1300s. One hundred years later, most of the New Testament and Psalms were translated by the Portuguese king, John I. Around 1644 a young Portuguese Protestant pastor, Joao Ferreira de Almeida, began trans-lating the New Testament. He continued translating Scripture throughout his lifetime and the Portuguese Bible was finally completed by a cohort of Dutch Reformed missionaries among Portuguese colonies in 1753. *The Almeida Version,* as it came to be known, had widespread popular use among Brazilian Portuguese speakers. During the twentieth century, several modern translations were done in Brazilian Portuguese to more closely reflect the language as commonly used there.

Not surprisingly, many Brazilian tribes neither speak nor read Portuguese. Also, regrettably, thousands of tribes were decimated by European diseases—significantly reducing the language diversity. Estimates of the current need for Bible translation in Brazil range between twenty and eighty languages. However, these estimates are often made by foreigners and do not reflect the perspective of the Brazilians. The actual need for Scripture translation may be much higher, as more than 180 languages are still spoken there today. Only three Brazilian languages have the complete Bible.

Our Connection

Paul Fahnestock worked in the family heating and air-conditioning business in Wichita, Kansas for sixteen years before entering seminary. He earned a Masters of Divinity, with an emphasis in missions, and a Doctor of Ministry degree. He became an ordained Presbyterian pastor. After completing seminary, Paul and Linda moved first to Uzbekistan, then later to Natal, Brazil as missionaries. Paul served as an evangelist, church planter, and taught at the Bible college. Naturally, they learned Brazilian Portuguese and made many friends during their years there.

When they returned to the U.S. in 2005 Paul began serving as Associate Pastor at the First Presbyterian Church in Bonita Springs, Florida. After living cross-culturally for seven years, Linda pursued a degree in English Language Learning.

In 2012 Linda heard about Wycliffe Associates' English Language Learning (ELL) program to serve Bible translators worldwide. She was so excited by the opportunity for cross-cultural ministry aligned directly with her interests and advancing Bible translation, she arranged for their church group to make the trip to Orlando to tour Wycliffe Associates and learn about volunteer opportunities. During the tour one of the specific opportunities highlighted was an upcoming ELL workshop—in Brazil. Linda enthusiastically volunteered to join the team, but the timing ultimately didn't work out for her to go on that trip. However, because of her background in Brazil, not long thereafter Wycliffe Associates' recruiters contacted Linda to ask her to consider serving as our Brazilian ELL Coordinator. She immediately agreed and led six ELL workshops there during the next two years. Paul accompanied Linda on a trip to encourage her. Through this involvement, they also got to know our Director of Education Services, Dan Kramer.

Paul soon found himself interested in another Wycliffe Associates strategy. In order to facilitate Bible translation into new languages, we had a team updating the 1901 American Standard Bible to create the Unlocked Literal Bible. This new resource would be released under Creative Commons licensing, enabling anyone in the world to use it freely for translation into any language without requiring copyright permission or payment. Paul was able to collaborate in this effort via the internet and helped to bring this valuable resource to completion in just over a year.

During the summer of 2014, Paul and Linda heard about a new Bible translation strategy called MAST that Dan was testing in the High Mountains. They saw my Facebook post asking how many translators it would take to translate the New Testament in two weeks. Paul and Linda thought, "If it's true, it's a game changer!" Upon Dan's return from the High Mountains, they heard his report firsthand. When the December 2014 workshop in the High Mountains completed half their New Testament, the Fahnestocks asked if they could participate in an upcoming workshop.

Anniversary Gift

By this time Paul had served on the First Presbyterian pastoral team for ten years. The church was looking for a way to express their appreciation for his service, so they sponsored Paul and Linda's travel to participate in the first

MAST workshop in Cameroon in February 2015. Dan led the workshop. Paul was the facilitator for the Weh translation team. Linda became the facilitator for the Mankon team that had come expecting to study their grammar—not to begin Bible translation.

Paul was curious to see how the experienced CABTAL exegetes engaged with MAST. He knew that their reaction would be an important indication of the potential future impact of MAST. The Cameroonian exegetes had good questions and a healthy skepticism, but Paul soon saw that as they worked through the eight steps of MAST they gained confidence. One of the exegetes, Eugene, was from the Weh language community. Within a short time, it was clear to Paul that the Weh team did not need him. If you think that Paul was disappointed by this you are wrong. Paul was excited to see firsthand that the MAST translation method worked. Once the translation team understood and applied the eight steps of MAST, there was no need for anyone to hover over them. The Holy Spirit was moving! Since the Weh team was making good progress, Dan took the opportunity to expand Paul's leadership experience by putting him in front of the group on the third day of the workshop.

Linda got to see the euphoria of the Mankon team as they began writing their language, and translating God's Word, for the very first time that week. It was beyond anything they could have imagined! As the first week of the workshop progressed they could not contain their excitement. They were anxious to bring the translation back to the Mankon church for their Sunday worship. Paul and Linda accompanied them on the weekend trip to their village. For the first time in their history, instead of reading Scripture in English and interpreting extemporaneously, the pastor read God's Word in Mankon! The congregation was elated!

During the second week of this workshop, Dan had to travel for another commitment. With Paul already taking increasing leadership responsibility, Dan asked him to coordinate the second week of the workshop!

As God worked *through* Paul and Linda to encourage Cameroonians to translate His Word, He was also working *in* the Fahnestocks—leading them toward a new ministry.

When Paul and Linda returned to Bonita Springs they told the story of what God had done in Cameroon, and that "God threw the door open" for them to help dozens of other languages have Scripture for the first time. Paul gave them notice that he would withdraw from the pastoral staff at the end of August.

Returning to India

In the 1960s a lot of people were searching for truth and meaning in their lives. Paul and Linda were no exception. Their search took them to India to study with a guru for six months. They learned yoga and meditation. They became vegetarians. They returned to the USA with this new knowledge but soon found it unsatisfying. They walked away from it all and began studying the Bible. God's Word changed their lives, but they always had a place in their hearts for India. Together they felt, "We owe India one."

As soon as the calendar turned to September the Fahnestocks were on a plane heading to India. They were scheduled to assist in four MAST workshops within six weeks. By the time they arrived, momentum was already building with MAST in India. They quickly learned that things in India happen on a totally different scale than in other places.

Their first workshop included fifty-two Indian translators from twenty-five different languages. Their second workshop included 147 translators working in thirty-seven languages. The facility for this workshop had no desks, so the translators worked using pens and tablets resting on their knees. The third workshop had thirteen languages. These three workshops all focused on translating Open Bible Stories—twenty-one Old Testament and twenty-nine New Testament Bible stories that tell key stories from Genesis to Revelation. For some of these languages, this was the first Biblical content they had. Other languages had portions of the New Testament, so the stories were their first Old Testament content.

The fourth workshop was for a language group of 34,000 people in extreme northeastern India. Twenty Christians came with a goal of translating at least one-third of the New Testament to take back to their people. By the time the fourth workshop wrapped up, Paul and Linda were exhausted.

Getting Closer to Brazil

After six weeks in India, the Fahnestocks flew from Delhi to Lusaka, Zambia. A New Testament translation workshop was planned for two languages. The Nkangala language team from Angola, another former Portuguese colony like Brazil, brought twenty-eight translators—including the Chief's extended family. Paul and Linda were back in their element communicating with the Nkangala team in Portuguese. The Luyana, from Zambia, had ten translators. By the end of the two-week workshop the Nkangala team had completed three-quarters of their New Testament, and the smaller Luyana team had completed one-quarter of theirs.

Brazilian-Portuguese Gateway MAST

One of the challenges to launching new Bible translations in Brazil is the copyright of existing Brazilian Bible translations. These cannot be used as translation sources without explicit permission. Since Paul had worked on the Unlocked Literal Bible English project he was already familiar with the solution to this problem—a strategy we call gateway language translation. Translating the Unlocked English Bible into the majority Brazilian-Portuguese would provide a valuable translation source for the remaining Brazilian languages, but in order to do that we would need a large team of Brazilian-Portuguese speakers. Their prior ministry experience in Brazil and Linda's involvement in English Language Learning positioned them to build partnerships with Brazilian churches for this effort. Paul and Linda traveled to Brazil in November of 2015 to visit six key cities around the country to recruit partners for the Brazilian-Portuguese gateway language strategy.

God's ways are often not our ways. Some of the partners that we expected to be enthusiastic about translating the Brazilian-Portuguese Unlocked Bible were not interested. However, other partnerships surfaced. Within two weeks the Fahnestocks gathered 150 names of Brazilian volunteers interested in working on this translation!

As 2016 began, Paul and Linda made plans for an initial gateway MAST workshop in the capital city of Brasilia during the first week of February. Thirty-one translators came to this workshop and completed translation of Matthew, Mark, John, Acts, Romans, 1 and 2 Corinthians, Galatians, Ephesians, 1 and 2 Thessalonians, 1 and 2 Timothy, Titus, Philemon, 2 and 3 John, Jude, and Revelation. That's 73% of the New Testament at the first workshop!

At two later Brazilian-Portuguese gateway MAST workshops in May, forty-six translators continued the Unlocked Literal Bible translation as well as beginning translation of the Unlocked Dynamic Bible—another open-license translation resource to assist translators as they tackle translation challenges.

So far more than 200 Brazilian translators and church leaders have given their time and talents to create Brazilian-Portuguese resources that local churches can use to launch Bible translation in every remaining language in Brazil. Several Brazilian church leaders have compared the Unlocked Brazilian-Portuguese Bible to other Portuguese Bible translations and have said, "The translation quality is excellent. We'll put it up against any Portuguese Bible."

Minority Languages

The first MAST workshop in Brazil for a minority language took place in September of 2016. An influential tribal group in northern Brazil sent sixteen translators to learn the MAST methodology and begin translating their New Testament. During the workshop, they completed Mark and Philemon, and they have continued translation in their home region. Once the open-license Bible translation resources are completely translated into Brazilian-Portuguese the door will be wide open for other minority languages to begin Bible translation for the first time.

Personal Testimonies

One of the many blessings that developed from the work on the Brazilian-Portuguese gateway translation was that God clearly called Brazilian leaders to a deeper commitment to Bible translation in minority languages. As the gateway translation teams worked, natural leaders and facilitators stood out. Others with specialized skills in information technology and audio or video recording stepped up. Everyone involved gained valuable experience using the MAST methodology and working as a team. Gateway translation quickly became their own strategy.

Denominational, tribal, and cultural differences disappeared when everyone was focused on Scripture. They said, "God is speaking in new ways!" While the new translation was the obvious goal, God was also working in the lives of the translators as they served. He was calling people deeper into ministry to their communities and their neighbors.

Translators described how God spoke to them personally as they spent long hours in His Word each day, calling them to a closer walk with Him. One translator was so moved by how God was touching her heart that she got out of her chair, knelt down on the floor, and began worshipping Him in the midst of the workshop. Another was so excited by new insights into his relationship with God while translating 1 John that he called his wife to join him for the second week of the workshop. He wanted her to experience the impact herself!

Monick

"The Psalmist David declares, 'Your eyes saw my unformed body. All the days ordained for me were written in your book before one of them came to be.' Psalm 139:16 NIV. I believe that the manner in which God led each one of us to MAST is a great miracle and demonstration of His sovereignty and love.

The gospel came to my family through a portion of the Bible. My great-grandfather, who was a coarse and gruff Italian immigrant, brought the Italian gospel of John with him to Brazil, read it, and was transformed by God. He passed the message on to my grandfather. I was not even born at the time, but the action of God in his life through a portion of the Bible had an impact that is reflected in who I am. Today I understand that the message that my great-grandfather received still needs to be taken to many other lives, and MAST is the tool that my Lord gave me to do this.

Many young people who have been willing to participate in MAST came with a fearful heart, doubting their ability to do something as meaningful as the translation of the Bible. This is exactly how I felt on my first day of translation. God taught me that it is He who has chosen us to do it. He showed me that we should not place our confidence in our own abilities and talents, but rather depend on Him alone. This fact, however, does not exempt us from our responsibility. Rather, it fills our heart with motivation for zealously seeking personal and professional improvement in order to work in the Lord's work.

When I reflect on what I have seen and lived in translation workshops I remember Paul's letter to the Philippians that teaches us about Christian unity and humility. As we translate we learn this in practice because we work collaboratively and for the same purpose. The methodology also leads us to submit humbly to each other since our work will be evaluated by other people. In MAST there is no room for standouts. We are all members of a body, working for the sole purpose of glorifying God.

As we work on the translation, God works in our hearts. We immerse ourselves in the Word of God in such a way that, at the same time we translate the Biblical texts, we are edified and transformed by the living and effective Word of God (Hebrews 4:12). At times we cannot contain our emotions and our eyes get wet.

MAST is the school in which the Lord has enrolled me to teach me some precious lessons. These lessons have had an impact not only in my life, but also on my family, friends,

and church. Now we understand more about the importance of God's Word for all ethnic groups."

Wellington

"After spending six years studying for the Bachelor of
Theology degree at the Baptist Seminary in Brasilia, I was
thinking about which ministry I would devote my life to.
At the time I worked as an advisor to the government, and
although it was good financially it was becoming a barrier
to ministry. I felt uncomfortable. After praying at the beginning of 2016, I asked to be dismissed from my employment
in the government, and I dedicated a period of time to prayer
only—seeking God's direction.

Then a friend told me about MAST. Before I had dreamed
of translating the Bible, but I felt unable to do so. However,
another friend went to a MAST workshop and encouraged
me saying, 'MAST tem a sua cara.' [MAST has your face.] He
meant I would be useful in the workshops. So, I accepted
the challenge.

It was love at first sight! When Pastor Paul talked about
the MAST method I started to cry, thinking that I would be
used by God to translate the Scriptures and thinking of the
size of the responsibility. During the last two days of the
workshop, Paul invited me, along with others, to review the
grammar. I loved it! In later workshops, we improved the
checking process.

I feel an enormous satisfaction working in the field where
I had prepared for so long—theology. And when I think of
the volume of work that will be done, I praise God for this.
Although we devote many hours of our day to our work, it
is so rewarding that my energies are renewed.

What I like most about the workshops is to spend the
whole day meditating in the Scriptures. Many times while I
check a text I learn new things about it, expanding my hori-
zons and letting God speak to me through His Word—which
is an inexhaustible resource. I have enjoyed this project
so much! At the moment my ministry is called MAST. My
top priority of service is this work that I love so much. This
work for me was God's answer to my prayers, and I praise

Him for it—to be part of this story. I intend to continue for many years—until all people have God's Word in their mother tongues."

Julio

"I have been a Baptist pastor for twenty-two years. I was a theology professor at the Theology Center of Vale do Paraiba in Sao Jose dos Campos, teaching classes in systematic theology, Reformed theology, contemporary theology, and Bibliology. I have always been zealous for the interpretation of Scripture, always seeking to make a Biblical exegesis within literal Biblical hermeneutics. In this, I have used my knowledge of original Biblical languages. After spending some time living in the United States, I returned to Brazil in 2015. By a sovereign act of God, I had not gotten a ministry position. This led me to raise various questions to the Lord because I could not understand why I was without a ministry. It was during this period that a dear couple invited me to participate in a MAST workshop. I decided to attend one of the MAST workshops without knowing for sure what I would find there.

What did I find? A receptive and cheerful environment. I was greeted by Paul and Linda Fahnestock. I found a group of Christians of different denominations and all with a common goal—to use their knowledge of languages to assist in the process of translating Scripture. I also noticed that the proposed method was simple to learn and execute, but that behind it was the commitment to make a faithful and understandable translation of the text. I also discovered that there was a commitment to revise the translation as needed, giving the project a serious character and commitment to the faithful interpretation of the Bible. There was a special zeal among the translators to remain faithful in every translated verse.

When this work is completed it will bless more than 450 indigenous languages throughout Brazil, of which more than 250 are eagerly awaiting the arrival of Scripture in their own language. The Unlocked Brazilian-Portuguese Bible will also reach other Portuguese-speaking nations: Angola,

Mozambique, Cape Verde, Guinea-Bissau, Sao Tome and Principe, and East Timor.

I never thought I would be used for such a magnificent work, but I was reminded of Paul's words to the Corinthians."

"Brothers, think of what you were when you were called. Not many of you were wise by human standards; not many were influential; not many were of noble birth. But God chose the foolish things of the world to shame the wise; God chose the weak things of the world to shame the strong. He chose the lowly things of this world and the despised things—and the things that are not—to nullify the things that are, so that no one may boast before Him." 1 Corinthians 1:26-29 NIV

Chapter Ten

DEAF OWNED TRANSLATION

L ook around your community. How many deaf people do
you see? It's a difficult question to answer because you
can't tell whether a person is deaf just by glancing at them.
They look just like everyone else. It's only when we take a
closer, longer, look that we begin to really see them. But
even when we look closely, it is difficult to understand the
differences between their world and ours.

Can You Hear Me Now?

Research by Gallaudet University estimates that around 600,000 people in the U.S. are functionally deaf. More than half of these are over sixty-five years of age, having lost their hearing late in life for a variety of reasons. This means that for most of their life they had functional hearing. They lived and learned in the hearing world. However, around 70,000 deaf Americans are under the age of twenty-one.

Think about this for a moment. This is a small fraction of a percent of the general population, but for deaf individuals this is the only world they know. Most of us have someone in our family who has difficulty hearing, but very few of us know someone who is deaf from birth. Many of our assumptions about the deaf are based on our experiences with people who were not actually born deaf. We unintentionally assume that their lives are very similar to ours. But they are not.

Try to imagine the world without sound. It's almost impossible for a hearing person to imagine. Without sound we would see and feel movement and vibration, but often it would surprise us. It might be in our peripheral vision, or behind us. People around us would move their mouths, but many dimensions of volume and inflection would be invisible to us. We would see signs, letters, words, and sentences as codes for objects, people, and actions around us, but would not know that others can understand them by hearing. We wouldn't even know what hearing is. We might assume that everyone lives in silence like us, except that it becomes painfully obvious that others are connecting in ways that we cannot. But even as we do this exercise, our imagination is distorted by our hearing.

But, have you noticed, the U.S. is not like much of the rest of the world? Today newborn hearing screening is common in the U.S. There are many educational options for the deaf in the U.S. that are far less common worldwide. In many countries the deaf are considered to be little more than wild animals, sometimes even cruelly kept in cages. They are considered cursed physically, and spiritually. Too often they are overlooked, marginalized, and excluded by the hearing world. For too long this has even been true in the world of Bible translation. Only American Sign Language has a New Testament translation.

A DOOR Opening

Wycliffe Associates has a long history of partnership with the Bible Translation and Literacy (BTL) Association in Kenya. They formed in 1981 to engage Kenyan Christians in Bible translation for all of the languages of Kenya. In the early 1990s, Wycliffe Associates partnered with BTL to begin development of their Ruiru Conference Center. Construction and expansion of this center was continuing when I came to Wycliffe Associates in 2000. In 2005 we partnered with BTL to build their new administrative offices in Nairobi. Their prior offices had been progressively damaged by earthquakes.

During these years we had several Wycliffe Associates staff living and working long-term in Kenya to serve BTL as well as other African partners in Bible translation. Around 2009 we began hearing of a new Bible translation partner working in several of the countries surrounding Kenya, Deaf Opportunity OutReach (DOOR). Then President of DOOR, Bob Buss, contacted us to discuss the possibility of building their Africa Deaf Bible Translation and Training Center in Nairobi.

As we discussed this project we were introduced to a world that we had unintentionally overlooked. At that time estimates indicated that there were more than four hundred unique sign languages in use worldwide. Four hundred! Equally shocking, we learned that not one of these sign languages has a complete Bible. Not one! Not even American Sign Language. At that point, Bible stories were available in several sign languages but hundreds of sign languages had no translation in progress—or even planned.

As we enthusiastically dove into the design and construction of DOOR's Bible translation center for Africa we also began supporting Bible translation in sign languages. Several of our staff were deeply moved as we learned more about the many obstacles to sign language translation and committed themselves to serving deaf communities full-time. We created a team to coordinate our support for sign language translation worldwide. In 2011 DOOR dedicated their Africa Deaf Bible Translation and Training Center, paving the way for more African sign languages to begin Bible translation.

Getting Started

As MAST expanded to serve oral languages questions inevitably surfaced about whether it could have a similar impact for sign languages. Dan began rallying people for a March 2016 initial test of MAST for sign language in Orlando. They recruited four deaf Americans to participate as translators, and invited Mirta Barreto, a Paraguayan leader in sign language Bible translation, to observe the test. The goal was to test the first four steps of MAST and test some ideas of how to record the video translations. During the first three days, Mirta was quiet. By the fourth day, she had drafted a plan to put MAST to work for seven sign languages in South America. She also agreed to join Dan and the MAST team for the first MAST sign language translation workshop overseas.

The first overseas MAST workshop for sign languages was planned for July 2016 in Cameroon. Two different deaf Cameroonian communities were invited to join seven hearing communities at this workshop. The CABTAL facilitators would lead the hearing translation teams. Dan Kramer would work with the sign language teams.

But as is often the case, God had a different plan.

Before Dan went to Cameroon, he led the first MAST workshop in the neighboring country of Gabon. Church leaders and translation teams from six Gabonese languages attended the workshop. God unexpectedly invited another leader who worked with the deaf community. When asked why she came she simply said, "The deaf need God's Word too!"

Fortunately, this leader in deaf ministry can hear, so she was able to easily follow along as Dan verbally introduced the eight steps of MAST to the other translation teams. Initially, she attempted sign language translation herself, but she quickly realized that it would be better to directly involve deaf people from the community. She invited deaf friends to the workshop. As they worked through the MAST steps, Dan video-recorded everything on his iPhone so that the files could be downloaded for later editing. During this two week workshop, the Gabonese sign language translation team completed the first five chapters of Luke. They were thrilled!

On to Cameroon

After the unexpected early launch of Deaf Owned Translation (DOT) in Gabon, Dan invited the Gabonese sign language facilitator to travel with him to Cameroon. Dan had also invited Mirta Barreto from Paraguay to attend. This proved to be a huge encouragement for both of them, and for the Cameroonian sign language translation teams.

Just as when working with translators who do not speak English, all of the instructions and discussion with the deaf translators took place through an interpreter. In this situation, the interpreter had to speak and understand English and also be able to sign in the local sign language. God provided local people with these skills to enable this to happen!

The first obstacle to overcome was the lack of video Scripture to use as a source text for translation. Deaf people are often unable to read and understand the spoken local languages. In this case one translation team included people who could read French, so a French Bible translated in 1910 became the initial source text. The other translation team included people who could read English, so they used our open-license English Bible source text. They read the assigned passage, then they signed the story to the other deaf translators.

One thing that quickly became apparent was that building understanding of the Biblical content took a lot of time and effort for those that could not read the written language. Also, sign language structure is very conceptual. A single sign may be used to translate an entire phrase. Finger-spelling is not usually preferred because too few deaf are literate in the local language, so it takes a lot of signed conversation to be sure that everything in the Bible passage is captured in the signed translation. One way the translators managed this was by using smaller chunks of Scripture for each segment of translation.

Once the translators understood the content, and they agreed on an appropriate way to sign it in their language, one of the translators did the memory draft. This was the equivalent of the blind draft for written translations. It challenged the translator to sign the content in a natural way, not stilted by constant reference to the source. A video studio, consisting of a wall covered with a green sheet, was improvised on the spot. These sign language translations were recorded using cell phones and digital cameras. Saving and tracking video segments had the same challenges we faced managing audio recordings. Plus, it required a lot more digital memory.

Each video segment then went through the same checking steps as written translations in order to assure quality, clarity, and naturalness—self-check, peer check, key-term check, and verse-by-verse check. As improvements were identified, new video recordings were made to capture the final translation.

By the end of the workshop, the sign language teams had translated several chapters in Mark. Dan was exhausted but exhilarated, and ready to put what he'd learned in Cameroon to use for other sign languages.

Building Our Team

As Deaf Owned Translation gained momentum God drew people into the team. Kaitlin Brown and Ashley Sell, both daughters of Wycliffe Associates staff members, were interested in sign language even though neither are deaf. Ashley invited Mike Geckle, a deaf member of her church, to join the team. Shelby Kania is another of Ashley's recruits. Our Chaplain, Mark Chapman, invited Brian Cross, the deaf pastor of the deaf congregation at their home church in Kentucky, to join the team. We hope to soon add a video technician and other international members to the team.

Brent's Personal Connection

About twenty-four years ago, a boy was born in China. The specifics of his earliest days are unknown, but some things are clear. He was born deaf, and as a very young child he was severely burned from his lower back and legs to his feet. His birth parents abandoned him to a government facility. His initial skin graft surgeries were done without anesthesia, and he recovered in an orphanage.

A few years later, Sammy was adopted by Pastor Dean and Cherie Ropp—Brent Ropp's brother and sister-in-law. As soon as he was in the U.S. the Ropps began the process of assessing and meeting Sammy's needs. After weighing various options, they chose to get Sammy a cochlear implant to give him some hearing ability. At first, he was confused and unhappy with the foreign object attached to his head. But over time he adjusted and began to learn how to understand the sounds he was hearing. Later, Sammy learned American Sign Language. Being surrounded by hearing people, he learned to read lips and connect the shapes with the sounds he could hear. When the time came for school, Sammy began attending the public schools in their community.

Two years after the dedication of the Africa Deaf Bible Translation and Training Center, Brent invited his nephew, Sammy, to travel with him to visit DOOR. This was the first time Sammy met deaf foreigners. Despite the sign language and cultural barriers, Sammy immediately connected with the deaf translators. Instead of feeling like a deaf person in a hearing world, he got a glimpse into the larger world of deaf people. It sparked an interest in his heart.

Needs in South America

After the successful MAST sign language workshops in Gabon and Cameroon, word began to spread among other Bible translation partners working in sign languages. Support for their work has been a chronic challenge because of the time and expense commitment required to accomplish the work. The interest in finding a more efficient means of doing Bible translation in sign language was high.

Workshops followed in India and Laos, launching sign language translation in their deaf communities.

Mirta Barreto is the Assistant Executive Director of LETRA Paraguay and is leading the sign language Bible translation effort there. She is also well-connected with sign language translation efforts by other Bible translation partners in South America. When she returned from Cameroon, she began inviting partners interested in sign language translation in six other South American countries to attend a January 2017 workshop: Bolivia, Brazil, Ecuador, Peru, Uruguay, and Venezuela. All six of these teams wanted to begin Bible translation. They had tried to start translating Scripture before, but always encountered obstacles that could not be overcome. Their hopes had been raised—and dashed—repeatedly. The host country, Paraguay, had already started sign language translation using traditional methods. This enabled them to assist the teams that were just beginning. Somehow word of this workshop spread all the way to South Korea. Three South Korean deaf pastors planned to attend and observe. They are connected with the Asia Pacific Sign Language Development Association (APSDA) linked to seventeen Asian countries—all still without sign language Scripture.

Back at Wycliffe Associates, interest in learning more about Deaf Owned Translation (DOT) was high. Our VP of Recruiting, Deborah Bartow, and our VP of Finance, Tim Neu, had served on several MAST teams but were anxious to see how it would work with deaf translators. Brent Ropp joined this MAST team as well, and invited his deaf nephew, Sammy, to assist. This was also the first workshop where Brent's son, Michael, began to take direct responsibility for leading DOT workshops.

Working Quietly

When everyone gathered in Paraguay the group included sixty deaf translators, their hearing Spanish or Portuguese interpreters, the Korean observers, and the American facilitators. Eighty people were packed into one room. Anticipation was high. As each team met others from new countries they exchanged greetings and immediately began crossing sign language barriers to communicate with one another. Smiles, waving arms, and poised fingers stirred the air. The hearing interpreters and facilitators joined the conversations in Spanish, Portuguese, English, American Sign Language, and Finnish Sign Language. Yes, Finnish SL. One of the workshop facilitators had learned to sign in Finland. The total was ten sign languages and three hearing languages!

Dan opened the workshop by speaking English instructions into a microphone. At his side, interpreters translated his English into Spanish and Portuguese. Then seven South American interpreters would sign the instructions into their country's unique sign language. Questions from the translators would be signed back to the interpreters for Dan's response. Yes, it was at least as complicated as it sounds. But the translators were focused and intent on learning the MAST method.

As always, the best way to learn MAST is by doing. They soon divided into their country groups and began consuming, expressing, chunking, and memory-drafting in front of the green screen and digital camera. Despite dozens of people signing simultaneously, the room was eerily quiet. Normally noise management is a major challenge at multi-language MAST workshops. But not this time.

About half of the deaf translators could not read. Many had very little formal education. American deaf are quite unusual in this regard, with more educational options. Some of the translators had grown up using unique signs and gestures they made up in their homes, so they struggled to understand the other sign languages. The deaf Christians all knew about Jesus, but few of them knew any Scripture. As a result, many of the South American deaf translators relied heavily on their hearing interpreters to read the source Scripture and sign it sufficiently until they could understand. Fully grasping the meaning of each passage required a lot of sign conversation before the translators were ready to attempt a memory draft in front of a camera. The first step, consuming Scripture, required a long time.

At this workshop, our team tested video recording using computer tablets and Videoshop editing software. It was better than Dan's iPhone but still needs improvement to be more usable by the local teams following the workshop.

Drafting from memory was very difficult for some of the teams. Unless the recording covered just a couple verses, key elements were inadvertently omitted. At one point the Venezuela sign language team had their hearing interpreter stand behind the camera to prompt them as they made their video draft. Not surprisingly, this resulted in very stilted and unnatural signing by the translator on camera. This experience reinforced the importance of doing this step from memory rather than while consulting a reference.

Once a video draft was completed, each segment was reviewed using the normal MAST process: self-check, peer check, key-term check, and verse-by-verse check. Because sign language is organized by thoughts or concepts, it is essential to ensure that no verse or detail is omitted in the summary. Final videos were recorded once the content had undergone all the checking steps. As the translators recorded the videos they began to gain more confidence and understanding of the whole process. But the time required to accomplish each step is much greater for sign language than either oral or written languages.

Many of the participants had previously given up on signing Scripture, thinking the best they could do was signing Bible stories. However, during this workshop, the new translation teams translated from two to six chapters of Mark. This was the first Scripture in history for these sign languages! The more experienced Paraguay team translated fifteen chapters in Exodus. The three South Korean pastors came as skeptics but departed as enthusiastic advocates.

Lessons Learned

In some ways, Deaf Owned Translation is very similar to both oral and written MAST. The breakthrough idea in every MAST workshop is that God has equipped the local church with the unique depth of language and cultural knowledge that enables them to steward God's Word for their own language and people. Minority language Christians no longer have to wait for majority language Christians to authorize their work. Oral cultures are no longer dependent on literate cultures. The deaf need not wait for the hearing. Each of these communities owns their translation. It is theirs—no one else's.

Every translator initially feels inadequate for the task. This is true of those who are formally educated as well as those who work in the marketplace. They recognize the holiness of God's Word, the eternal implications of their work, and their own unworthiness. This is true for hearing and deaf translators. But the context of life as a deaf person harshly reinforces their marginalization. They learn early, and often, that they are misfits in a hearing world. So the experience of successfully translating Scripture for their deaf community is intensely rewarding. When God speaks through their hands—it changes the way they see themselves. They see themselves through His eyes.

One counterintuitive lesson from Deaf Owned Translation is that the deaf are actually better communicators than most hearing people. When hearing people from different languages, like English and Mandarin, meet it is very difficult for them to understand anything. The sounds, cadence, and tones are unrecognizable. When deaf people meet, even from different sign languages, their experience in decoding movements from hearing communities gives them an advantage in interpreting the signs of another language. Crossing this sign barrier isn't daunting to them. They connect and communicate much more quickly than hearing people speaking different languages.

Another lesson, less surprising but perhaps more challenging, is that sign language translations are still going to require more time and expense than oral or written translations. We are continuing to search for ways to overcome these challenges, but are also committed to persevering to see that every deaf community in the world has God's Word in their own sign language. Only God can make this happen.

Their Plans

The seven South American sign languages are planning to reconvene to continue their New Testament translations.

Word of what happened in Paraguay is spreading, so it would not be surprising to see other deaf translators, or even hearing translators, show up to launch translation in their languages. In principle, there is no reason not to combine hearing and deaf translations at a single workshop. They certainly won't disturb one another!

The Korean pastors said, "Thank you so much! Our eyes are opened. We didn't believe this was possible, but now we've seen it. We are going home to tell our people. We will invite you to come and have an event in South Korea for Asian languages."

Mirta said, "I am sure what we accomplished in this event would have taken at least ten years to accomplish without MAST."

After DOT

Gathering deaf Christians together is, unfortunately, a rare event. When it does happen, it can make a huge impact in the deaf community.

During a DOT workshop in Laos, Brian Cross and Mike Geckle had the opportunity to preach in sign language in a local church. They had picked up enough Laotian Sign Language, supplemented by their own American Sign Language, to communicate the gospel message. At the end of their workshop, Thai deaf translators put together a Christmas program for their community. Eighteen deaf attendees gave their lives to Christ as a result!

During a DOT workshop in India, Brian led devotions for the group, clearly presenting the message of salvation through Jesus Christ. He contrasted the many languages in the world with the only true salvation in Christ. Three of the deaf translators who were from Hindu families gave their lives to Christ. They knew that their decisions would cost them dearly. They knew that they would likely face beatings and abuse from their families and neighbors because of their decision. But they chose Christ instead of the approval of others.

Following the DOT workshop in Paraguay, the translation team from Venezuela reported their progress to their congregation at the First Baptist Church in Maracaibo. For the first time in the church's history, a deaf person preached to the entire congregation. This was a breakthrough for the community as a deaf person overcame their shyness to preach boldly, and as the congregation responded to the message. As they showed videos of sign language translation of Mark, many could not contain their tears. Several deaf responded by putting their faith in Christ during this service!

Each of these deaf communities is continuing to move forward with Bible translation, knowing that it will require perseverance, but believing that both the short-term and long-term results will be a blessing for their people.

New Research

Many deaf people learn to communicate as children in the homes of families that do not know the local sign language. This results in unique Home-sign language that does not reflect sign usage by others outside the home. Academic research on Home-sign is increasing, but the almost infinite variations in gestures and meanings pose a major challenge for Bible translation in home sign languages.

One of our hearing-impaired team members, Emily Wang, recently began testing the potential to use pictographs as symbols for key theological terms in Scripture. We call this Symbolic Universal Notation (SUN). The initial study of the first four chapters of Mark yielded seventy two symbols required to convey key-terms. Reading these symbols in sequence as they occur in Mark, readers were able to produce an understandable English back-translation! One participant said, "It reads like the New Living Translation!" Additional symbols are being tested to serve as modifiers to the primary symbols to convey intensity, dimension, pace, or other language features. The goal is to create pictographs that Home-signers can understand. Obviously, a lot more testing is needed to determine the feasibility of this approach for translating Scripture.

Reflections

Brent has been to multiple MAST workshops around the world. He's seen them in Asia, Africa, and South America. He has observed and facilitated. He led an oral MAST workshop in India, with his family helping to facilitate. As moving as each of these experiences has been, there was something unique about the Deaf Owned Translation workshop. "Six deaf people groups, who did not have a single verse of Scripture, now have multiple chapters of Mark in their sign languages. Is it perfect? I don't know because I don't sign their languages. What I know is that their pastors were involved, are still part of the translation team, and they are thrilled to have their first Scripture. If they later see ways to improve the translation, they have the means to revise and update it. They can work in their deaf communities. They can communicate with other pastors in their communities to improve the translation. The point is, before they had nothing. Now they have started the gospel of Mark, and soon we believe they will have more. They want to continue translation because they want more than Mark. They want the whole Bible."

I asked Brian, Mike, and Sammy, our deaf translation teammates why it is important for the deaf to have their own Bible translations. Brian's response was profound. He signed, "Because it is important to God."

His response left me speechless. In the midst of this work, it is easy to be overwhelmed by the complexity and challenges and to wonder whether it is worth the effort. But ultimately it is God's heart to reveal Himself to all people— not just hearing people or literate people. He knows us and wants us to know Him. It is important to Him.

Sammy said, "So many deaf people don't have the opportunity to learn about Jesus. Others have seen preaching about Jesus, but know nothing about the rest of God's Word."

Mike signed, "The deaf need the help of the hearing. We need encouragement and support."

Taken together, the approximately seventy million deaf people of the world are the largest unreached people group today. They need God's Word in every sign language.

Chapter Eleven

VIRTUAL MAST

After growing up in the era of cold war between the United States and the Soviet Union, it is hard to believe that the USSR broke up more than a quarter century ago. In the early 1990s, I traveled to Russia and Kazakhstan to establish transportation and communication strategies to serve an increasing number of Christian missionaries moving into the region. During the late 1990s, I made my first visits to Central Asia. In 2010 Wycliffe Associates began supporting Bible translation in the Caucasus region, a linguistically diverse area of the former Soviet Union. By the time MAST emerged in 2014 we had developed a network of partners in this region that quickly became interested in putting MAST to work for local languages. How that happened is another story of God's providence.

A Unique Start

Dima was born in Tajikistan in 1979. His father is Muslim. His mother is Russian Orthodox. Both were communists. Dima is none of those.

During the Soviet years, Dima's mother worked as a bookkeeper in a state-owned factory. After the breakup of the Soviet Union, ethnic and religious strife boiled over into a civil war. The only work she could find was as a waitress in a restaurant. Times were hard for Dima's family.

Into this turbulent world came an unexpected distraction—video games. The first places Dima saw these were at video game rooms. They typically had several desks with televisions and Sony game consoles. People paid for an hour of playing time. Dima was one of the players. He loved the games, but he was also intrigued that this kind of business could generate income in the midst of such financial difficulties.

Purchasing a Sony PlayStation was impossible for Dima, but he was convinced that he could generate income for his family with a game room in his neighborhood. He convinced his mother to invest in his first company. She provided the capital to purchase a used PlayStation. They moved their appliances onto their apartment balcony and moved their couch and black and white television to make a game room in their kitchen. Dima recruited his grandmother to time the players and collect their money. Dima and his brother were the salesmen, recruiting all of their friends to come and play. The income from Dima's business helped his family through some difficult financial times.

Coming to Christ

Besides playing video games, Dima was a talented basketball player. By the time he was nineteen he was playing for Tajikistan's national team. Things were going well for him until one day he developed a severe pain in his stomach. He needed surgery to repair an injury, and afterward the doctors told him he could no longer play basketball. To Dima, it seemed like the end of the world.

Since he couldn't work with his body, he needed to work with his mind. He decided that learning English would be a good investment for future business. He found an English tutor and spent his entire savings of fifty dollars on English lessons. Unfortunately, his savings only lasted for one week of lessons. Once again, he felt beaten and discouraged. In his frustration he cried out to God, "If you exist, please help me with English!" A few days later his mother met someone offering English lessons for free.

Dima was anxious to resume his learning. The teacher said that someone would come to his apartment to pick him up for lessons. When Dima answered the door he was shocked to see a well-known neighborhood thug standing there. He suspected that these would not be fun English lessons, but he went along anyway. There was no way for Dima to know that the thug had recently given his heart to Christ.

After the English lessons, the group leader began reading from a Russian Bible. Dima asked if he could stay to listen. The discussion that followed was not actually a Bible study, but was a Campus Crusade training session for "How to reach everyone for Christ in Tajikistan." Dima listened.

A week later his new friends invited him to an outreach event at a place in the mountains. Dima invited ten of his friends to come along. It was the first time Dima heard the gospel given to a large audience. After explaining the gospel, the evangelist asked if anyone had any questions. Dima said, "I am a young man. Why should I follow Christ now?" The evangelist responded, "Because the days are evil, and you never know when your last day will come."

That night Dima took his mattress up to the roof of the building to be alone with God. Dima asked Christ to be his

Savior. When morning broke, and Dima awakened, he was surprised to see that he was not alone on the roof—all of his friends had also spent the night up there. Dima has been following Jesus ever since.

New Business Ideas

A few years later a friend asked Dima to help him create a website for his business. He had never done it before, but he figured he could learn. He soon found that he could make good money doing this, so he formed a company to design business websites. He also began using his new talent to help churches and Christian ministries build their websites.

In the midst of this, he had the idea to create a site to make Scripture freely available online for everyone in Central Asia. After creating the website he began contacting Bible publishers to put their Bibles on the site. He was shocked to learn how few Central Asian languages had Scripture, and that the Bibles which did exist were all copyrighted. The owners would not give him permission to publish their Bibles online. He was disappointed that his website had nothing to offer. With some research he learned that there were foreigners translating Scripture into Tajik. They estimated that it would take ten years to finish the New Testament. Dima was deeply frustrated but didn't know how to proceed.

God Builds the Team

One of the ways Wycliffe Associates began supporting Bible translation in the Caucasus was by recruiting volunteers to fill high-priority jobs for partners there. Rick and Cindy Gray were part of our Recruiting team, helping to match volunteers with the best overseas service opportunities. As Rick was speaking with people about the needs in the Caucasus, he sensed that God was calling him to go. So, in 2010 Rick and Cindy moved to the Caucasus. In the coming years, two things happened. First, they fell in love with the people. Second, they learned a lot about the urgent need for Bible translation in dozens of languages in the Caucasus region.

As we increased our support for Bible translation in this region we also learned of similar needs in nearby Central Asia. In 2011 we began partnering with a translation company owned by Tajik Christians. The next year a new Marketing Director, Dima, joined that company.

Around this same time, Eric and Judy Steggerda attended a Wycliffe Associates fundraising event in Florida. As they heard about the global needs for Bible translation, and the way that volunteers were filling key positions in the team, they too sensed God calling them overseas. They moved to the Caucasus as business consultants for the Tajik translation company.

During the next few years, we experienced an extraordinary number of challenges working in this region. At the same time, new partnerships developed and locations were identified that increased our freedom and flexibility to support Bible translation there.

Dima's Dream

"I dreamed that I saw a room. There was a table, and around the table were four sofas—wide sofas—and they were empty. Nobody was sitting on those sofas. I was sitting on another sofa, and I saw on the table different types of teapots, different shapes.

Each was different. I was surprised because in my culture I know how teapots look, you know. But why so different? Different styles. Then I saw people coming to sit down around this table and drink this tea. I recognized them. Then I saw other people who I didn't recognize. In the beginning they were friends I recognized, and then new people. It was an interesting dream, but I didn't understand it."

Local Church Perspective

Foreigners have been doing Bible translation in this region long enough to have completed New Testaments in a few local languages. This region has a centuries-long history connected with Scripture. Mount Ararat is here. Babel was nearby. Christianity became the state religion in Armenia at the beginning of the fourth century. The Bible has existed for more than two hundred years in majority languages here.

Inevitably, new Bible translations in minority languages are examined by bilingual church leaders in comparison with long-accepted majority language Scriptures. Unfortunately, translations by foreigners sometimes compare quite poorly.

Dima said, "I've been in meetings where church leaders and pastors shared their frustration with translations that were done by foreigners. They said, 'We can't poison our churches with this translation because it is not acceptable. We don't accept it.' I saw that with my own eyes. Then I remember when the church found sixty-four mistakes in Matthew and said, 'Please correct these mistakes, otherwise we will not use your Bible.' The foreign managers said, 'Okay. We will consider correcting these mistakes.' But I asked, How long will it take? They said, 'We don't know. Maybe six months. Maybe a couple of years.' But if you give this to the church they will correct it right away because they found these mistakes."

This was hard for me to hear. I know that Bible translators have sacrificed a lot to get God's Word to the people in this region. I know that they have spent years diligently studying the languages, drafting and checking their translations, in order to produce the highest quality result. But the reality is that the local people understand their language in ways that no foreigner can. The local church is the primary stakeholder in any Bible translation and is best able to judge the accuracy in their language. They feel the urgency and priority for their people. They live with the results in their communities.

New Optimism

As Dima was working with our Wycliffe Associates team, and as MAST emerged, he heard it described as a church-centered approach to Bible translation. It struck a chord with him. It was something he had already heard in conversations with local churches. "Foreigners decide how to translate the Bible. We would like to decide." Dima also heard foreign translators talk about a future time when the local church could do the translation, but they saw that as a distant future. His friends said, "We dream of doing translation with our local church. We are the local church!" When Dima heard Brent Ropp, Wycliffe Associates' VP of Operations, describe this as a current reality—he was thrilled! "I can't believe what I hear! It's amazing! It's great!"

"As an entrepreneur, as a Christian businessman, I understand that the Bible is the foundation for all ministries. So, I used to organize my games, sports events, and outreaches. These were great. But the Bible is the foundation. If I disappeared, the Bible would stay. It doesn't depend on me."

Dima was ready to experience church-centered Bible translation firsthand.

A Different Approach to MAST

Available source texts for translation are always an essential question to answer before any MAST workshop. Copyrighted translations cannot normally be translated without explicit permission and payment of royalties to the copyright owner. This is why Wycliffe Associates launched our open-license Bible strategy. Our team took the 1901 American Standard Bible, now in the public domain, and revised it to reflect current English usage—with the specific intent to make it understandable to people for whom English is a second language. This solves the problem of English Bible source text but does not immediately solve the problem for people who are not bilingual in English. Most of the people in the Caucasus region are bilingual in Russian. So, we recruited Dima to lead the translation of the open-license English Bible into Russian. This gave him a perfect opportunity to learn about MAST.

The challenge Dima faced immediately was finding people bilingual in English and Russian. Most of these are young people who are working full-time and cannot take two weeks off of work. Most of the older people, who might have available time, do not speak or read English. Dima's creative mind began thinking about ways for young people to collaborate online after work. Online crowd-sourcing strategies for writing computer code have been used to design computer games for years. Why not use this same approach for Bible translation?

Dima said, "I have been a developer since 2003. I've made many websites for businesses and churches. But I have a passion to do something bigger for the kingdom of God. Something with more impact." He asked Dan Kramer, "Is it possible to bring the MAST method to an online platform?" Dan admitted, "I have no idea." Dima then asked, "Can we try and see?" Naturally, Dan said, "Sure!" So Dima invited another programmer, Max, to collaborate in building an online tool that would allow the church to steward Bible translation for themselves—anytime and anywhere.

The Design

The idea is to include all of the eight steps of MAST in an online software that guides and supports the translation process. In addition to the software, translators and facilitators can connect using video or chat functions to answer questions or collaborate on a specific step. The end result is an integrated translation and project management tool called Virtual MAST (V-MAST). In order to get to step two, you have to complete step one. Every step that requires collaboration requires at least two people to sign off before the translator can proceed to the next step.

All that is needed to access the V-MAST software is an Internet connection, a browser, and password authorization. The password assures that, for security and quality-control purposes, everyone working on a translation in progress is known to the rest of the team. Once the translation has gone through all eight steps of MAST it is uploaded to a digital publishing website. All of the translations are published under Creative Commons open licensing, enabling anyone who speaks the language to access the translation without cost or limitation. No one will ever have to pay to read these Scriptures!

Initial Testing

Dima and Max worked on the initial design for V-MAST in early 2016. Translating our open-license English Bible into Russian provided a good way to begin testing the software. Dima recruited four Russians, all bilingual in English, from four different countries for the initial test in May 2016. He decided to facilitate the virtual meeting from our office in the United States so that other members of our MAST team could observe.

Prior to the meeting, Dima sent each translator their login credentials and password. Inside the V-MAST software, he had already assigned each of them a chapter in 2 Timothy to translate for the test. Four chapters, four translators. Dima opened the meeting with prayer, then another MAST facilitator, Paula, described the eight steps of MAST and the related software functions to them. Within just a few minutes, the translators began learning by doing.

As they worked, a dashboard in the software gave Dima and Paula the ability to watch the progress of each translator. They could see what each translator did on their own, as well as how they were collaborating with each other on shared steps. After a couple hours of work, Dima surveyed the translators to get their feedback and to hear their plans for progressing through the translation. Each translator would have their own schedule and pace of working. If anyone ran into a problem or delay, it would be visible to Dima and Paula on the dashboard. That would cue them to contact the translator by email or Skype to see how they could help them overcome the challenge.

After the May test, Dima organized a live MAST workshop in the Caucasus during July. This gave him the opportunity to see the workshop approach firsthand, and to encourage the growing Russian translation team. Seventy-five translators from fifteen countries came to this workshop! They included pastors, ministry leaders, and mature believers from many different churches. Some came from countries where Christians are monitored and persecuted. Others that wanted to come were unable, due to security problems in their countries.

Based on the feedback from the May test, and things learned at the live MAST workshop in July, additional testing was done in August and September of 2016. Each time adjustments were made to the user interface and software programming to simplify it and streamline the translation process. The Beta version of V-MAST went live in January of 2017.

Beyond the Dream

"When we started to work on V-MAST, my dream became a reality. Because who actually supported V-MAST in the beginning? They were my friends. Now new people are joining, and doing this stuff, and so excited to be part of this."

As the software has been used, Dima has gotten a lot of good feedback from the translators. One issue that surfaced is the need for a version that can be downloaded to use offline in places where the internet is either unreliable or not secure. Testing is underway for a version that will run on a secure local network. Once the translation is ready to publish it can be sent out of the country on a flash drive to upload to a web site.

Just as in live MAST workshops, the need to support oral translations will likely shape future developments of V-MAST. Audio collaboration tools will be added to the software.

One of the ways that V-MAST is complementing live MAST workshops is by networking the translation teams and church leaders after the workshop. This enables them to benefit by including additional church leaders who were unable to attend the live event.

During March of 2017, Max and Paula traveled to the Philippines to introduce V-MAST at a live workshop with ninety translators from nine languages participating. The live workshop gets the translations off to a strong start, builds enthusiasm, and introduces translators from diverse geographic areas. V-MAST will then enable them to stay connected and continue their work in the months ahead. Translation teams that finish their New Testaments can work on their Old Testaments using V-MAST. Max and Paula are also training the Information Technology team from Wycliffe Philippines to provide technical support and training for V-MAST locally.

Looking Forward

What does Dima's family think of what he is doing? His wife, Anna, is totally supportive of his work. She was one of the Russian translators in the first test of V-MAST in May of 2016 and is on the team continuing to translate the open-license Bible into Russian. Interestingly, she has a university degree in English and is learning the English Language Learning program that Dan originally created so that she can take it back home to the Caucasus. Dima's brother, Artem, has been helping check the Russian translation of our open-license Bible. His mother and father see the changes that faith in Christ has made in Dima's and Artem's lives. They see Christ in their attitudes and actions and encourage them in their Bible translation work.

Dima has a lot of ideas about how to continue improving V-MAST so that it can benefit translations teams globally. "I never say, 'We can't do that.' Instead, I say, 'How can we do that?' If helpful technology already exists, we can apply it to Bible translation."

Why should geography keep people from collaborating in Bible translation? Why should work or school schedules limit participation?

They should not, and do not.

Postscript

A GLOBAL MOVEMENT

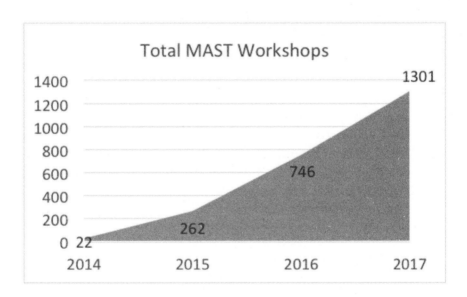

As I write this, it's been three years since a small group of Christians pioneered a new approach to Bible translation in the High Mountains of Asia. Since then, several hundred churches worldwide have launched 950 Bible translation projects using MAST. Another 199 projects are currently in various stages of planning. This pace of Bible translation expansion is unprecedented. It reflects the convergence of the global Church's spiritual maturity, their thirst for God's Word, and their readiness to invest the time, talent, and treasure God has entrusted to them.

As great as our rejoicing is that thousands of churches have launched Bible translation in their local languages, our hearts break for thousands more who have not even a single verse of Scripture.

In recent Wycliffe Associates strategic planning meetings. we prayed and reflected together on how to make MAST, and every other Bible translation resource, freely accessible to churches in every language. By God's grace, in recent years the time and financial cost of Bible translation has plummeted. But the cost is still out of reach for thousands of churches worldwide. Until the cost can be further reduced, Bible translation remains highly dependent on Western financial resources. We live with this reality even as we work to further reduce the costs.

Our goal is to soon reach the point that churches worldwide have every resource they need to effectively steward God's Word in their languages. This will allow all of the languages currently without Scripture to immediately begin translation. This will very likely be a higher number of languages than researchers previously estimated as churches evaluate language needs based on their local perspectives. At the same time, translations that were completed decades, in some cases centuries, ago also need to be revised in order to reflect changes in language use. The same training and tools that are being used to launch Bible translation in new languages will also equip churches to revise translations when appropriate.

Bible translation is becoming a movement of the global Church. The Reformation that Martin Luther began 500 years ago is finally reaching to the ends of the earth. The role of cross-cultural missionaries, including Bible translators, is increasingly shifting from pioneering in unreached people groups to serving the local church. Much of the skill and experience missionaries gained in recent decades is directly applicable to the ongoing work of Bible translation, but new skills are also required. In frontier missionary work, where no local church exists, foreign missionaries are the only church authorities. But working where the local church has already been planted and grown means serving in submission to local church authority. This transition from foreign to local church authority is already underway. It presents a learning opportunity for each of us.

Some people ask me about the future of MAST. I'm not a prophet but I do have visibility to some of the current trends. Churches worldwide have embraced MAST quickly and it appears that this trend will continue for the foreseeable future. MAST empowers local churches to control their own access to Scripture. After generations without God's Word, this is a welcome change for them. Progress in translating Bible translation resources into gateway languages means that people bilingual in any of these fifty major languages will soon have access to valuable translation tools.

MAST is also increasingly being contextualized by local churches. It looks different in Cameroon than it does in the Philippines. Partners modify MAST to suit their local needs. It is being called by new names in new places. All of this is encouraging to me. MAST is not a trademark or franchise that we are trying to control and license. It is a strategy to serve and empower the Church to translate Scripture for themselves. It is possible that within a few years MAST will be a forgotten acronym. It may be replaced by French, Mandarin, or Arabic acronyms. It will certainly grow, change, and adapt as old challenges are overcome and new challenges surface. Our goal is not to defend or preserve MAST, but to see God's name exalted among the nations through His Word.

I began this book by reflecting on the miraculous healing of the blind man in John 9. To me this continues to be a helpful lens for understanding what God is doing through MAST. At the same time, I know that there are others who do not share this perspective.

I'm reminded of the concerns that surfaced when Jesus's disciples were performing miracles after Pentecost. In Acts 5 the disciples were called to account for their actions by the spiritual leaders of the community. As the leaders considered their options, a man named Gamaliel offered wise counsel. He said that if the disciples' actions were simply human efforts they would inevitably fail, but that if they were of God they would certainly succeed.

This is my prayer regarding MAST. If it is simply human effort, let it clearly fail. If it is of God, may it abound with all honor and praise to Him.

MAST REACHING THE NATIONS

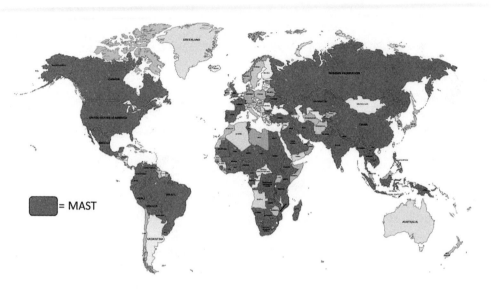

= MAST